LEARNING THE LANGUAGE OF
AUTISM

AN **A-TO-Z** GUIDE FOR PARENTS AND TEACHERS

VERONICA CRAFTON

TO:_______________________________

FROM:_____________________________

Learning the Language of Autism

An A-to-Z Guide for Parents and Teachers

Copyright © 2024 by Veronica Crafton

ISBN: 979-8-218-46424-0

Book Editor: Bianca Frails

Book Design & Layout by: Kantis Simmons, The SIMAKAN Group

www.VeronicaCrafton.com

Dedication

This book is dedicated to all the incredible parents and teachers I've had the privilege of working alongside over the years. Your dedication, compassion, and unwavering support inspire all I do.

Table of Contents

Acknowledgements

First and foremost, I extend my deepest gratitude to my parents, family, and the family I've made along the way who have been my unwavering support system. Your belief in my vision and your endless encouragement have been my foundation.

Former students, past and present clients, and the many children I've met along the way, thank YOU. I've learned more from you than any book, class, or CEU. Thank you for your patience with all of us as we try our best to help you reach your goals.

I am immensely grateful to the Amazingly Uplifted team. Words cannot express my appreciation for all you do for the children we serve. Thank you for not only understanding the mission but helping fulfill the vision.

A special thank you to my mentors whose insight and guidance have been invaluable. Your wisdom and patience have helped shape my thoughts, shape my purpose, and execute my visions.

I am also grateful to the many parents and teachers who shared their stories and experiences. Your openness and perseverance have been the bedrock of this project. You remind me every day of the impact we can have when we come together with a common purpose.

And to all my friends who provided feedback, encouragement, and much-needed breaks from the writing desk, thank you. I am so blessed to have such compassionate, thoughtful, caring, and genius friends!

Introduction

In 2006, fresh out of college and brimming with excitement, I began my first job at a private facility dedicated to children with autism and other severe developmental and behavioral challenges. I felt an undeniable surge of anticipation, eager to finally make a meaningful impact in my new professional life. One of my first clients was a bright-eyed two-year-old girl. Her mother shared that she had been developing typically but started regressing in her development shortly after her 2nd birthday. She'd lost her speech completely and was mute.

Working with her over the next few months was transformative. She began saying words, then short phrases, and eventually formed full sentences. She even started becoming more conversational, slowly regaining her language skills. Though my time at that job was brief—only a year—I kept in touch with her family. Later, when she was in elementary school, her mother asked me to tutor her. By that time, she was enrolled at a local public school in a general education, co-taught classroom. I worked with her once a week on her math homework.

Throughout elementary and middle school, her mother ensured she received the necessary support and services. She was a relentless advocate, even enlisting specialists to attend Individualized Education Program (IEP) meetings to secure her daughter's needs. As high school approached, her mother found a private school that seemed like a perfect fit. Her daughter thrived because of her dedicated teachers and the intentional relationship they built with families. And the cherry on top: the once mute little girl graduated as valedictorian of her class.

I was honored to attend that graduation alongside her family. Seeing her go from being mute to the valedictorian filled me with pride. Knowing the struggles she faced and overcame brings a smile to my face every time I think of her, her mom, and teachers!

Imagine a parent witnessing their typically developing child suddenly lose all their speech. (I realize that some of you parents can.) It's devastating. Yet, despite the initial heartbreak, this mother remained resolute, advocating for her daughter and securing the support she needed to make tremendous progress. Along the way, dedicated teachers also provided invaluable guidance. There were teachers that saw her potential. Without their dedication and initiative, the girl may have had a very different experience in school and in life.

I share this story as a testament to the power of collaboration between parents and teachers. That's the essence of this book. It's for parents and teachers because it takes both to help a child truly thrive. When parents and teachers work together, speak the same language, and share the same intention and passion for the child's success, remarkable things happen.

How to Use This Book

Learning the Language of Autism is designed to help parents and teachers of children with autism through information, implementation and inspiration.

It will help you understand commonly used jargon like dyspraxia and acronyms like IEP, FBA, and DTT. I remember my first year of teaching like it was yesterday. I was overwhelmed and felt completely clueless when it came to the special education "alphabet soup". Parents have also shared that when their child was diagnosed there was little to no education on what to expect or what they needed to know. This book provides an abundance of information to help you learn the basics along the way.

Information is great but implementation can be even better. Some of the key terms come with implementation strategies for parents to use at home *and* teachers to use at school. I also encourage parents and teachers to share strategies with one another to help the child with generalization (don't worry, "generalization" is on page 104).

Hard days are inevitable. On those days crack this book open for a little inspiration. Feeling down, read "Optimism". Feeling hopeless, read "Believe". Feeling like you don't know what you're doing, read "WTF". These and many other entries sprinkled throughout the book were written to encourage and uplift you on those not so sunny days.

Read it straight through, skip around, or pick it up when you need it. Take notes along with way and you'll be ahead of the game!

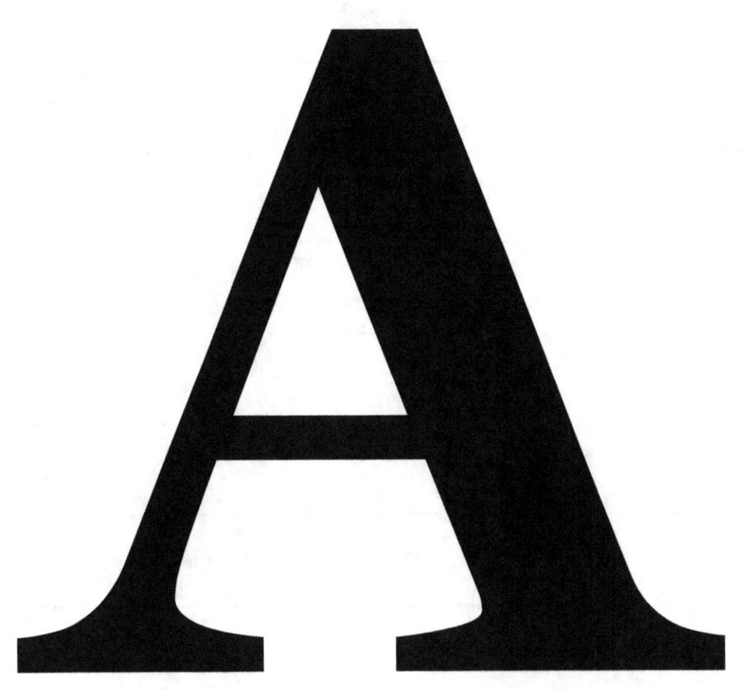

NOTES

Autism

Autism, or Autism Spectrum Disorder (ASD), is a neurodevelopmental disorder characterized by challenges in communication, social interaction, and restricted or repetitive behaviors. It's called a "spectrum" disorder because the specific symptoms and the severity of those symptoms can vary broadly from one individual with autism to another[1]. Let's look at the three key indicators:

1. Communication Difficulties: One hallmark of autism is communication challenges. This can manifest in various ways, such as delayed speech development, difficulty understanding and using language, or limited use of gestures and nonverbal communication. Some individuals with autism may have a rich vocabulary but struggle with pragmatic language skills, like taking turns in conversation or understanding sarcasm and idioms. Others may have echolalia, where they repeat words or phrases without understanding their meaning. These communication difficulties can lead to frustration and isolation for individuals with autism, as they may struggle to express their thoughts, feelings, and needs effectively[2].

2. Social Interaction Challenges: Individuals with autism often struggle with social interaction. They may find it difficult to understand social cues, such as facial expressions, tone of voice, or body language, which are crucial for effective communication. As a result, they may have trouble forming and maintaining relationships, making friends, or engaging in reciprocal conversations. For instance, a person with autism might avoid eye contact, have difficulty initiating conversations, or struggle to understand the perspective of others.

3. Restricted and Repetitive Behaviors: Individuals with autism often engage in repetitive behaviors or have narrow, intense interests. These behaviors can include repetitive movements (such as hand-flapping or rocking), insistence on sameness or routines (becoming upset by changes in their environment or daily schedule), or preoccupation with specific topics or objects. For example, a person with autism might spend hours organizing objects in a particular way, focusing intensely on a single subject, or becoming distressed if their routine is disrupted. These restricted and repetitive behaviors can serve as coping mechanisms for managing sensory sensitivities or anxiety, but they can also interfere with daily functioning and social interactions.

While there are common characteristics and traits associated with autism, it's crucial to understand that there are no characteristics that are unique to autism alone. Many behaviors and traits associated with autism can also be present in individuals without autism, and vice versa. Additionally, autism is a spectrum disorder, meaning that individuals with autism can vary widely in terms of their strengths, challenges, and abilities. Therefore, it's important to avoid making assumptions or generalizations based on stereotypes and to approach each individual with autism with understanding, empathy, and respect.

If parents suspect that their child may have autism, it's essential to take proactive steps to seek guidance and support. Here's a roadmap for what parents can do:

1. Trust Your Instincts: Parents are often the first to notice if something seems different about their child's development. Trust your instincts if you suspect that your child may have autism. Don't dismiss your concerns, even if others suggest waiting or downplay your observations.

2. Consult with Healthcare Professionals: Schedule an appointment with your child's pediatrician or family doctor to discuss your concerns. Be prepared to provide specific examples of your child's behavior or developmental milestones that you find concerning. Your healthcare provider can conduct a preliminary evaluation and may refer you to specialists for further assessment.

3. Seek a Comprehensive Evaluation: If your healthcare provider recommends further evaluation, seek out specialists who have experience in diagnosing autism spectrum disorder. This may include developmental pediatricians, child psychologists, or neurologists. A comprehensive evaluation typically involves a combination of observations, interviews, and standardized assessments to assess your child's social communication skills, behavior, and developmental milestones.

4. Explore Early Intervention Services: Regardless of whether a formal diagnosis of autism is made, early intervention is critical for supporting your child's development. Early intervention services, such as speech therapy, occupational therapy, and behavioral therapy, can help address your child's specific needs and promote their communication, social interaction, and adaptive skills.

5. Connect with Support Groups and Resources: Seek out support groups and resources for parents of children with autism. Connecting with other parents who have been through similar experiences can provide valuable emotional support, practical advice, and resources. Additionally, organizations or local autism advocacy groups may offer information, workshops, and community events.

It's also important to recognize what autism isn't. Autism is not a result of poor parenting nor is it a disease that can be cured. Instead, it's a neurodevelopmental condition that is present from early childhood and affects individuals throughout their lives. With appropriate support and intervention, individuals with autism can lead fulfilling and meaningful lives.

AAC Device

An AAC device, short for Augmentative and Alternative Communication device, helps individuals who struggle with verbal communication. These devices range from simple picture boards to advanced computer systems and apps that generate speech. AAC devices are life-changing for people with speech and language impairments[3].

Imagine an AAC device as a personal DJ for words: users select symbols, pictures, letters, or words, and the device transforms these selections into spoken language. It's like putting together a puzzle to express thoughts, needs, and feelings. For some, it's like texting but with speech output—talking through technology!

Speech-Language Pathologists (SLPs) are crucial in setting up AAC devices. They determine which device will be most helpful, customize it for the child's needs, teach them how to use it, and work with families and teachers to support communication in all environments. This teamwork combines expertise and patience to enhance communication skills[4].

For parents, integrating an AAC device at home offers a fantastic opportunity to improve communication in a familiar setting. Use the device during meal times, story reading, and play activities, making it a natural part of the child's day. By consistently modeling how to use the device, parents help their children become more skilled at expressing their wants, needs, and feelings. It's not just about giving voice to thoughts—it's about building confidence and strengthening family bonds through better interaction[5].

At school, teachers can use AAC devices to create a more inclusive and interactive classroom experience. Picture a classroom where every student can express their thoughts and participate in discussions, regardless of their verbal abilities. Teachers can integrate AAC technology into group projects, class discussions, and individual presentations. This promotes an environment where all students feel valued and heard. Using AAC devices in classrooms also helps peers communicate more effectively with classmates who use these tools, fostering empathy and cooperation.

ABA Therapy

ABA therapy, or Applied Behavior Analysis therapy, is a scientific approach to understanding and changing behavior. It involves teaching new skills and reducing behaviors that may be harmful or interfere with learning. ABA therapists use various techniques, such as positive reinforcement, to encourage positive behaviors and discourage negative ones[6].

Parents can access ABA therapy for their children through several avenues. They may seek services from private ABA providers, schools, or educational programs that offer special education services incorporating ABA principles. Some health insurance plans may also cover ABA therapy, and government-funded programs or agencies may provide services to eligible children with developmental disabilities.

ABA principles can be effectively applied in classroom settings to support students with autism and other developmental disabilities. Teachers can create individualized learning plans based on students' specific needs and strengths, using techniques such as task analysis and prompting to break down skills into manageable steps. Positive reinforcement motivates students and encourages desired behaviors. Teachers can also use ABA strategies to manage challenging behaviors, teach social skills, and collect data to track progress and adjust instruction as needed6. ABA therapy can be a valuable tool for both parents and educators in promoting the learning and development of children with autism.

It's important to note that ABA has evolved significantly over time. While early methods were criticized for being too rigid or punitive, modern ABA is more flexible and person-centered, focusing on positive reinforcement. There's a greater emphasis on understanding the individual's needs and incorporating their interests into therapy. The goal is to help individuals unlock their potential and lead fulfilling lives7.

Accommodations

Accommodations are changes in the learning environment or teaching strategies that allow a children access the curriculum and demonstrate their learning more effectively. They do not alter the content or expectations of what the child is expected to learn but rather provide different ways for the child to engage with the material and show their understanding. Accommodations are vital because they level the playing field by ensuring they have the same opportunities to succeed as their peers. These adjustments can help reduce barriers related to sensory sensitivities, communication challenges, and difficulties with flexibility and adaptability. By addressing these barriers, accommodations can improve the child's ability to participate in classroom activities, focus on tasks, and achieve academic goals.

Determining which accommodations are appropriate involves a collaborative process between parents, teachers, and specialists. This process includes observing the child in different settings, identifying specific challenges, and considering the child's strengths and preferences. For example, if a child has difficulty processing verbal instructions, providing written instructions or visual supports might be beneficial. It's important to regularly review and adjust accommodations to make sure they continue to meet the child's evolving needs.

While accommodations change how a child learns, modifications change what a child is expected to learn. Modifications involve altering the curriculum content, expectations, or assessment criteria to better match the child's abilities. For instance, if a child with autism struggles significantly with grade-level math, a modification might involve providing them with a simplified math curriculum tailored to their skill level. Both accommodations and modifications are important tools in an IEP, but they serve different purposes in supporting the child's educational journey.

Americans with Disabilities Act (ADA)

The ADA, or Americans with Disabilities Act, is a landmark civil rights law enacted in 1990 that prohibits discrimination against individuals with disabilities in all areas of public life, including jobs, schools, transportation, and public and private places open to the general public[8].

For parents of children with special needs, the ADA is both a shield and a tool, providing protection and empowerment. Here's what they need to know:

1. Equal Educational Opportunities: The ADA ensures that children with disabilities have the same opportunities to learn as their peers, including access to public schools, reasonable accommodations, and the right to an appropriate education tailored to the child's needs.

2. Reasonable Accommodations: Schools must provide accommodations to special needs students. This could include assistive technology, modified learning materials, or physical accessibility changes in the school.

3. Protection Against Discrimination: The ADA shields children from discrimination based on their disability, ensuring they are not excluded from educational opportunities.

4. Advocacy and Legal Support: If a child's rights under the ADA are violated, parents can seek legal recourse. This law empowers parents to advocate for their child's needs.

5. Transition Services: For older children, the ADA helps in preparing for life after school, including higher education and employment opportunities, paving the way for a bright and independent future.

The ADA is more than just a law; it's a right to inclusion, equity, and access. It empowers parents to be the champions their children need, ensuring that the playing field is not just level but also welcoming and inclusive. Familiarizing yourself with the ADA will help you be a stronger advocate for your child.

Adaptive Skills

Adaptive skills are essential tools for children with autism, helping them navigate the world with confidence and independence. These skills, encompassing everyday tasks and behaviors, are crucial for fostering self-sufficiency, enhancing social integration, improving overall quality of life, and reducing family stress. Teaching these skills ideally begins as soon as a child is diagnosed with autism[9].

Teaching adaptive skills involves breaking down complex tasks into smaller, manageable steps, maintaining consistency and routine, using visual aids for better comprehension, and employing positive reinforcement to encourage and celebrate achievements. Modeling these skills and providing regular practice opportunities is also beneficial. When choosing which skills to teach, it's important to assess the child's individual needs and strengths, focus on age-appropriate skills, prioritize safety and health, and consider the child's interests to keep the learning process engaging. Professional input from teachers and therapists can also guide the selection of beneficial skills[10].

Monitoring and adapting the teaching approach based on the child's progress is key to effective learning. This approach involves observing which strategies are most effective and making adjustments as needed. Each small step forward should be celebrated, as these skills gradually build up, equipping the child for a more independent and fulfilling life. This process is not just about skill development; it's about preparing the child for life's adventure, making their journey smoother and more enjoyable[11].

Adulthood

The transition to adulthood for autistic individuals is a journey filled with both challenges and opportunities. As young adults with autism approach adulthood, the focus shifts towards fostering their independence and autonomy. While ongoing support may be necessary, the ultimate aim is to empower them to make informed decisions about their lives, including choices regarding living arrangements, education, and employment.

Transition planning typically begins during middle or high school, encompassing the development of self-advocacy skills, setting realistic goals, and exploring career interests. Continued education may involve vocational programs, community colleges, or universities. Parents should collaborate with educators to identify suitable post-secondary programs and supportive resources. Autistic individuals possess strengths that can be harnessed in various job roles[12].

Housing decisions are significant for adulthood. Some autistic individuals thrive in independent living situations, while others may prefer residing with family members or in supervised housing settings. Parents should explore housing options well in advance, considering supportive living arrangements like group homes or supportive independent living when necessary.

Financial planning is another critical aspect of preparing for adulthood. Parents need to explore legal mechanisms such as guardianship and conservatorship if required, while also establishing special needs trusts to safeguard their child's financial well-being. Familiarity with government programs like Supplemental Security Income (SSI) and

Medicaid is essential for accessing crucial financial support[13].

The transition to adulthood for autistic individuals demands careful planning and unwavering support. Parents and teachers play pivotal roles in facilitating this transition, offering guidance, advocacy, and a nurturing environment that empowers autistic individuals to embark on a fulfilling journey into adulthood. Each individual's path is distinct and filled with potential for growth and achievement.

Advocate

Advocacy is crucial in ensuring that children with autism receive the support and resources they need to thrive academically, socially, and emotionally.

For parents, advocating for their children involves being their voice and championing their rights within educational settings and beyond. This includes:

1. Understanding Rights and Resources: Parents should familiarize themselves with laws and regulations governing special education services, such as the Individuals with Disabilities Education Act (IDEA)[14]. Knowing their child's rights empowers parents to advocate effectively for appropriate educational accommodations and services.

2. Building Collaborative Relationships: Establishing positive relationships with teachers, school administrators, and other professionals involved in their child's education is essential. Effective communication and collaboration facilitate the development of individualized education plans (IEPs) and enable the child's needs to be met.

3. Providing Information and Documentation: Parents should gather relevant information, such as medical records, evaluations, and assessments, to support their advocacy efforts. Clear documentation of their child's strengths, challenges, and educational goals can inform decision-making and advocacy strategies.

4. Attending IEP Meetings: Active participation in IEP meetings allows parents to contribute to the development and review of their child's educational plan. They can share insights about their child's progress, goals, and preferences, and also collaborate with the IEP team to address any concerns or challenges.

5. Seeking Additional Support: Parents can seek support from advocacy organizations, support groups, and legal professionals specializing in special education law. These resources can provide guidance, information, and assistance in navigating complex advocacy issues.

For teachers, advocacy involves promoting the educational needs and rights of their students with autism within the school community. This can include:

1. Understanding Students' Needs: Teachers should take the time to understand each student's unique strengths, challenges, learning styles, and preferences. This enables them to provide individualized support and accommodations that promote student success.

2. Collaborating with Parents and Professionals: Building positive partnerships with parents, special education staff, therapists, and other professionals that support the child is essential for effective advocacy. Unified teamwork ensures that students' needs are addressed comprehensively and consistently across settings.

3. Providing Differentiated Instruction: Teachers should employ instructional strategies that accommodate diverse learning needs and preferences. Differentiated instruction allows students with autism to access the curriculum at their own pace and in ways that suit their learning styles.

4. Creating Inclusive Learning Environments: Teachers can foster inclusive classroom environments that celebrate diversity, promote acceptance, and encourage peer interactions. Creating opportunities for socialization and collaboration helps students with autism feel valued and included in the school community.

5. Advocating for Resources and Support: Teachers can advocate for additional resources, training, and support services to meet the needs of students with autism. This may include requesting specialized training, assistive technology, or access to behavioral supports within the school setting.

Overall, effective advocacy by parents and teachers is a critical measure that enables students with autism to receive the support and opportunities they need to reach their full potential. By working collaboratively, advocating for their rights, and implementing evidence-based practices, parents and teachers can create inclusive educational environments where all students can thrive.

Anxiety

Many individuals with autism experience anxiety, and it can manifest in various ways. Some common ways in which individuals may experience anxiety include heightened sensitivity to sensory stimuli, difficulty with transitions or changes in routine, and challenges in understanding and navigating social situations.

Sensory overload can be a common trigger. Imagine being in a bustling, noisy place where every sound and sensation is intensified—it can be incredibly distressing and overwhelming. Additionally, navigating social interactions can be complex, leading to social anxiety or difficulty in understanding others' emotions and intentions.

Here are some ways parents and teachers can help a child that may be experiencing some anxiety:

1. Open Communication: Foster open and empathetic communication. Create a safe space where they feel comfortable expressing their feelings and concerns. Let them know that it's okay to talk about their anxiety. If they are non-verbal place a heavy emphasis on teaching emotions. Visual emotional scales, social stories, and visual cues can be immensely helpful for children with autism. These tools provide structure and predictability, easing anxiety related to transitions and new experiences.

2. Sensory Management: Be mindful of sensory sensitivities. Certain environments may trigger anxiety. Provide tools like noise-canceling headphones or sensory toys that can help them self-regulate.

3. Social Skills Training: Consider enrolling in social skills training programs. These can help them better navigate social situations, reducing anxiety related to social interactions.

4. Establish Routine: Maintain a consistent daily routine whenever possible. Predictability can be comforting and reduce anxiety related to unexpected changes.

5. Self-Care: I can't stress this enough! Remember that taking care of yourself is crucial too. Parenting and

educating a child with anxiety can be challenging, so make sure you have a support system in place and take breaks when needed.

Remember what works for one may not work for another. It's essential to tailor your approach to specific needs and preferences. With patience, understanding, and the right support, you can help manage their anxiety and thrive.

Apraxia

Apraxia, specifically Childhood Apraxia of Speech (CAS), is a motor speech disorder where children have difficulty planning and coordinating the movements required for speech. This condition is not due to muscle weakness or paralysis but rather a disconnect between the brain's signals and the muscles involved in speaking. Children with apraxia know what they want to say, but their brains struggle to direct the necessary mouth and tongue movements to produce the correct sounds in the right order.

Apraxia can occur independently, but it is also relatively common among children with autism. Studies suggest a significant overlap, with a notable percentage of children with autism also being diagnosed with Childhood Apraxia of Speech. This co-occurrence can complicate both diagnosis and intervention, as the symptoms of autism and apraxia may intersect and influence one another.

Both autism and apraxia contribute to communication difficulties, but in different ways. Autism often affects social communication skills, such as understanding and using nonverbal cues, engaging in reciprocal conversations, and grasping the nuances of social interactions. On the other hand, apraxia specifically affects the ability to articulate speech sounds and form words correctly. When a child has both conditions, these communication challenges can be more pronounced, requiring specialized approaches to support their speech and language development.

Addressing apraxia in children with autism involves tailored intervention strategies that consider both the motor speech difficulties and the broader communication challenges associated with autism. Speech-language therapy is crucial, with a focus on repetitive practice and multi-sensory approaches to help the child develop the motor planning skills needed for speech. Therapists may use techniques such as visual and tactile cues, prompting, and augmentative and alternative communication (AAC) systems to support the child's ability to communicate effectively.

Assessment

Assessments for children with autism encompass a range of evaluations designed to serve distinct purposes in understanding and supporting their development. These assessments can be broadly categorized into three types: diagnostic assessments, skills assessments, and behavior assessments.

Diagnostic assessments are conducted to determine whether a child has Autism Spectrum Disorder (ASD) and to comprehend the nature and extent of their symptoms. Trained professionals such as psychologists, developmental pediatricians, neurologists, or psychiatrists typically administer these assessments, utilizing tools like the Autism Diagnostic Observation Schedule (ADOS) and the Autism Diagnostic Interview-Revised (ADI-R).

Skills assessments, on the other hand, aim to evaluate the child's current functioning levels across various domains, including cognitive abilities, language skills, motor skills, and adaptive behaviors. These assessments may involve standardized tests like the Vineland Adaptive Behavior Scales and are administered by professionals such as speech and language therapists, occupational therapists, psychologists, or special education experts, depending on the specific area being assessed. ABLLS, AFLS, and the VB-Mapp are some other frequently used assessment to determine a child's skill set.

Each type of assessment plays a crucial role in building a comprehensive understanding of a child with autism. Diagnostic assessments establish the presence of autism, skills assessments provide a baseline of the child's abilities, and behavior assessments aid in creating targeted intervention plans to address specific behavioral challenges. This collaborative effort involving various professionals ensures that the child receives tailored support that aligns with their unique needs and abilities.

Assessments used for children with autism in schools encompass a variety of domains tailored to the child's age, developmental stage, and specific needs. These assessments serve to identify strengths, challenges, and areas requiring support to inform educational planning and intervention strategies. Developmental assessments evaluate a child's milestones across domains such as communication, social skills, motor skills, and cognition, utilizing tools like the Mullen Scales of Early Learning and the Bayley Scales of Infant and Toddler Development. Cognitive assessments, such as the Wechsler Intelligence Scale for Children (WISC), gauge intellectual functioning and cognitive abilities, while adaptive behavior assessments, like the

Vineland Adaptive Behavior Scales, measure independence in daily life activities.

Language and communication assessments, including the Peabody Picture Vocabulary Test (PPVT) and the Clinical Evaluation of Language Fundamentals (CELF), evaluate language skills comprehensively. Social skills assessments, such as the Social Skills Improvement System (SSIS), focus on social functioning and interaction abilities. Behavioral assessments, including Functional Behavior Assessments (FBAs), explore behavior patterns, sensory sensitivities, and emotional regulation. Additionally, transition assessments assist in identifying a child's strengths, preferences, and interests as they transition from school to post-school activities. These assessments are important for developing Individualized Education Programs (IEPs) or 504 plans tailored to meet the unique needs and goals of children with autism. Qualified professionals, such as school psychologists and special education teachers, conduct assessments with cultural sensitivity and comprehensive understanding to ensure effective support and intervention strategies for each child.

Assistive Technology (AT)

Assistive technology (AT) can be a big game-changer. It can empower individuals with disabilities to overcome barriers, fostering independence, and enhancing their quality of life. It can be immensely helpful in education by providing alternative means of communication, facilitating access to information, and accommodating diverse learning styles. For example, a child with autism who has difficulty with verbal communication might benefit from using a speech-generating device that allows them to express their needs and participate in classroom discussions. Similarly, a student with autism who finds transitions challenging can use visual schedules to understand and anticipate daily routines, reducing anxiety and improving focus. These tools not only support learning but also boost confidence and engagement by helping the child communicate more effectively and feel more in control of their environment.

The process of determining whether a child needs assistive technology is a collaborative effort involving educators, parents, specialists, and the student themselves. It begins with a comprehensive assessment of the student's abilities, challenges, and individualized goals. This assessment takes into account the nature of the disability, the specific tasks or skills requiring assistance, and the environment in which the technology will be used. Key factors in determining the need for AT include the student's ability to access the curriculum, communicate effectively, and participate in classroom activities. If the assessment reveals that the student's disability significantly impacts their ability to achieve these goals, AT is considered.

Additionally, legal requirements, such as those outlined in the Individuals with Disabilities Education Act (IDEA) in the United States, mandate that schools *consider* AT as part of the Individualized Education Program (IEP) planning process for eligible students. AT should be viewed as a potential solution when traditional methods alone are insufficient to support the student's educational needs.

NOTES

Baseline

A child's baseline establishes a reference point to track progress or the effectiveness of interventions for a child with autism. In the realm of data collection, especially concerning present levels of academic performance and behaviors, establishing a baseline is essential. It serves as a foundational reference point, providing crucial information about the frequency, intensity, and duration of specific behaviors or academic abilities before any interventions are introduced. Without this baseline, accurately measuring progress becomes challenging, as there's no starting point to gauge improvement from. Every goal should have a clearly stated baseline, as it enables educators, therapists, and parents to tailor interventions precisely to the child's needs. In essence, the baseline acts as a fundamental benchmark, ensuring that progress is measurable and interventions are effective in supporting the child's development.

BCBA

A Board-Certified Behavior Analyst (BCBA) is a highly trained professional who specializes in applied behavior analysis (ABA) therapy, particularly in working with individuals with autism spectrum disorder (ASD) and other developmental disabilities. To obtain their credentials, individuals must complete a master's degree in a related field (such as psychology, education, or applied behavior analysis), complete specific coursework in behavior analysis, obtain supervised experience in the field, and pass a rigorous examination administered by the Behavior Analyst Certification Board (BACB)[15].

BCBAs play a crucial role in helping children with autism by designing and implementing individualized behavior intervention plans (BIPs) tailored to each child's needs. These plans focus on teaching new skills, reducing challenging behaviors, and promoting social interactions and independence6. BCBAs utilize evidence-based strategies grounded in the principles of behavior analysis to assess behaviors, identify underlying factors contributing to those behaviors, and develop interventions to address them effectively.

In addition to working directly with children, BCBAs can also provide valuable support and guidance to parents at home. They may offer parent training sessions to teach effective behavior management techniques, offer strategies for promoting skill development and communication, and provide support and encouragement to parents navigating the challenges of raising a child with autism. By empowering parents with the knowledge and tools they need, BCBAs can help create a supportive home environment conducive to the child's growth and development.

In schools, BCBAs play a vital role in supporting students with autism and other developmental disabilities. They collaborate with educators, administrators, and other professionals to assess students' needs, develop individualized education plans (IEPs) or behavior intervention plans (BIPs), and provide training and support to school staff on implementing evidence-based strategies. BCBAs may also conduct functional behavior assessments, analyze data, and monitor progress to ensure that interventions are effective and that students are making meaningful gains in their academic and social skills.

Behavior

Behavior is a powerful form of communication, and for children with autism, it's often their way of expressing needs, desires, and emotions. Autism encompasses a wide range of behaviors and characteristics, from challenges in social interactions to repetitive behaviors and intense sensory sensitivities. At home, parents may observe their child struggling with making eye contact, engaging in reciprocal conversations, or exhibiting repetitive behaviors like hand-flapping or adherence to rigid routines. Some children with autism may also display maladaptive behaviors, such as aggression, self-injury, or sensory overload.

In schools, teachers may notice similar behaviors, such as difficulty with social interactions, adherence to routines, or sensory sensitivities that impact the child's learning and participation in classroom activities. Recognizing that all behavior is a form of communication is crucial for both parents and teachers in understanding and addressing the needs of children with autism.

Seeking professional guidance and therapy is essential for addressing these behaviors with sensitivity and directness. Applied Behavior Analysis (ABA) therapy offers structured interventions tailored to the child's individual needs, helping to promote positive changes in behavior. Additionally, creating a sensory-friendly environment both at home and in the classroom can help alleviate sensory sensitivities and provide a more comfortable space for the child to thrive.

Patience and persistence are key as parents and educators work together to support children with autism. It's important to be open to trying various strategies and to seek support from autism support groups or professionals when needed. Embracing the real-world application of these techniques and adapting them to the child's specific needs can make a significant difference in their progress and well-being.

Parents and teachers navigating the challenges of supporting children with autism, know that you are not alone on this journey. While the topic of severe behavior in autism may feel isolating, it's essential to remember that progress, no matter how gradual, is worth celebrating. Take proactive steps to ensure the safety of both yourself and the child by identifying triggers, having regulation strategies readily available, and establishing an emergency intervention plan at home and school[16].

Behavior Intervention Plan

A Behavior Intervention Plan, or BIP, is like a personalized roadmap designed to help a child with autism navigate challenging behaviors and promote positive ones. It's typically needed when a child exhibits behaviors that interfere with their learning, social interacted crafted specifically for your child's specific needs. It consists of several key elements. First, there's a clear description of the challenging behavior. The definition should be clearly written with examples and non-examples of the behavior. Then, it outlines specific strategies and interventions for everyone who works with your child to follow. These strategies should be evidence-based and individualized, considering your child's strengths and challenges.

Creating a BIP involves a collaborative effort. A student's team – including parents, teachers, and professionals – works together to design and implement the plan. It's essential for everyone to be on the same page, to provide consistency and support across all environments. Data collection is a crucial aspect of a BIP. Collecting data helps monitor the effectiveness of the interventions and allows for adjustments when necessary. It's a way to confirm that the plan is working to improve your child's behavior and quality of life. Data sheets can be shared weekly so that parents are aware of the effectiveness of the interventions.

Parents can also expect teachers and service providers to implement the BIP with dedication and care. The team should provide ongoing communication, sharing updates on progress and addressing any concerns promptly. Regular meetings to review the BIP and make necessary adjustments are also a part of the process. Parents should feel empowered to ask questions, share insights about their child, and be active participants in the journey towards positive behavior change[17].

Believe

Believing in a child with autism is not just about having faith in their potential—it's about recognizing and celebrating their strengths, talents, and capabilities. When parents and teachers believe in a child with autism, they convey a powerful message of acceptance, support, and encouragement. Equally important is believing in oneself as a parent or teacher. It's about acknowledging the challenges, embracing the journey, and trusting in one's ability to make a positive difference in the child's life. Parenting or teaching can be both rewarding and challenging, but having belief in oneself is like having a guiding light in the midst of uncertainty. It's about recognizing one's strengths, seeking support when needed, and never underestimating the impact of love, patience, and perseverance.

When parents and teachers believe in both the child and themselves, magic happens. It creates an environment where the child feels valued, understood, and empowered to reach for the stars. It fosters a partnership between home and school, where everyone works together to support the child's growth, development, and success. So, let's hold onto that belief—the belief in the incredible potential of every child with autism and the belief in our own ability to make a difference in their lives.

Body Language

Body language is a universal form of communication and is especially important for children with autism. Being aware of your own body language can significantly impact your interactions with them. Start by maintaining an open and friendly posture—avoid crossing your arms or showing tension. This can create a warm and inviting atmosphere[18].

Eye contact might be difficult for some children with autism, but avoiding it doesn't mean they are uninterested or disrespectful. Instead, focus on listening attentively and showing engagement through your facial expressions. A genuine smile can help build trust and connection.

Consistency in body language is crucial because children with autism often thrive in structured and predictable environments. Your consistent gestures and expressions can make them feel safe and secure. Additionally, respect their personal space and boundaries since some children might be sensitive to touch or proximity. Pay attention to their comfort level and adjust accordingly[19].

Most importantly, practice patience and empathy. Take the time to observe and understand their cues, and be flexible in adapting your communication style to meet their needs. Remember, your body language conveys acceptance, understanding, and support, which are essential for fostering positive connections that help children with autism thrive and express themselves in their own way.

Bonding

Building strong bonds with children with autism is a journey that requires patience, understanding, and genuine connection from both parents and teachers alike. One of the most powerful ways to bond with these children is by engaging in activities that they enjoy and find meaningful. Whether it's playing with a favorite toy, exploring a shared interest, or simply spending quality time together, finding common ground creates a foundation for deeper connection.

Communication is another key aspect of bonding. Recognizing and respecting their preferred mode of communication is essential. Some children may prefer nonverbal communication, such as using pictures or gestures, while others may respond well to verbal communication with additional support. Adapting your communication style to meet their individual needs fosters mutual understanding and strengthens the bond between you.

Consistency and predictability are also vital for children with autism. Establishing routines and sticking to them provides a sense of stability and security, helping them feel safe and understood. Positive reinforcement, such as praise, rewards, or preferred activities, can further motivate and reinforce desired behaviors, deepening the bond between parents, teachers, and the child.

Patience and flexibility are fundamental when bonding with children with autism. Building trust and connection takes time, and it's essential to be patient and understanding along the way. Embracing progress, no matter how small, and remaining flexible in your approach demonstrates your commitment to their well-being and strengthens the bond between you.

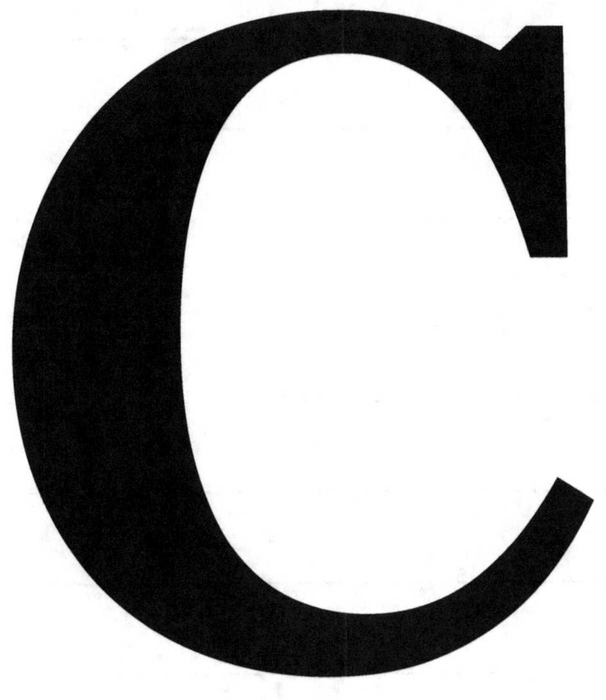

NOTES

Can't vs. Won't

Understanding the difference between a child with autism not doing something because they aren't capable and not doing something because they don't want to is necessary for providing effective support and intervention. When parents and teachers accurately distinguish between these two scenarios, they can tailor their strategies to the child's needs. If a child's inaction is due to a lack of capability, the focus can be on skill-building and providing necessary supports. Conversely, if the issue is related to willingness, interventions might involve motivational techniques or addressing underlying emotional or sensory issues. Misinterpreting a child's behavior can lead to inappropriate interventions, causing unnecessary frustration and a negative learning experience.

Recognizing the root cause of a child's behavior fosters respect and empathy, showing the child that their unique challenges are acknowledged and valued. It also improves communication, encouraging open dialogue about the child's preferences and capabilities, leading to more effective and supportive interactions. This understanding empowers the child by providing the right tools and encouragement, which can boost their confidence and sense of accomplishment. It also helps prevent frustration by setting realistic expectations and avoiding repeated failures that could lead to a sense of helplessness.

In practical terms, regular observation and assessment are vital in understanding a child's abilities and preferences, combined with open dialogue with the child and their caregivers to grasp any underlying factors influencing their behavior. Flexibility in adapting strategies based on ongoing observations and feedback is key to effectively meeting the child's evolving needs. By distinguishing between incapability and unwillingness, caregivers and educators can create more inclusive, supportive, and empowering environments for children with autism, fostering their development and participation in a positive and meaningful way.

Communication

Children with autism often face significant challenges in communication, spanning a spectrum of physical and social difficulties. Verbal communication may be delayed or absent, making it challenging for them to express their thoughts, feelings, and needs through spoken language. Nonverbal communication, such as gestures, facial expressions, and body language, may also be limited, hindering their ability to understand social cues and interact with others effectively. These challenges can impede a child's ability to communicate their true intellect, as their cognitive abilities may far surpass their ability to express themselves verbally or nonverbally[20]. It's crucial not to equate an inability to communicate with lower intelligence, as many children with autism possess remarkable cognitive abilities that may be masked by communication difficulties.

Speech-language therapists are trained to help children improve their communication skills. These professionals specialize in assessing and treating communication disorders, including speech and language delays, and social communication difficulties. They also work closely with children with autism to develop individualized treatment plans tailored to their unique needs and strengths. Additionally, behavioral therapists and occupational therapists may also play a role in supporting communication development, providing targeted interventions and strategies to enhance communication skills in various contexts[21].

By recognizing the diverse challenges children with autism face in communication and the importance of providing specialized support and intervention, we can create inclusive and supportive environments where every child has the opportunity to communicate, connect, and thrive. Here are some strategies that may be useful at home or in the classroom:

1. Create a Structured and Predictable Environment: Establishing routines and providing a predictable environment can reduce anxiety and help children with autism feel more comfortable and secure, facilitating communication.

2. Use Visual Supports: Visual aids such as picture schedules, visual timetables, and social stories can help children with autism understand and navigate daily routines, express themselves, and comprehend social situations.

3. Encourage Alternative Forms of Communication: For children who struggle with verbal communication, explore alternative forms such as sign language, picture exchange systems (PECS), typing, or augmentative and alternative communication (AAC) devices to empower them to express themselves effectively.

4. Provide Clear and Concise Language: Use simple, concrete language and avoid abstract concepts or figurative language that may be confusing. Be direct and specific in your communication.

5. Model Social Skills and Communication: Demonstrate appropriate social skills and communication behaviors through modeling. Use verbal and nonverbal cues to teach turn-taking, initiating and maintaining conversations, and understanding social cues.

6. Practice Patience and Empathy: Communication difficulties can be frustrating for children with autism. Practice patience, empathy, and understanding, acknowledging their efforts and providing support and encouragement.

7. Create Opportunities for Communication: Provide ample opportunities for children to communicate (verbally or nonverbally) throughout the day, incorporating communication into everyday activities and routines.

8. Utilize Specialized Therapies: Work with speech-language therapists, occupational therapists, and other professionals trained in autism intervention to develop individualized treatment plans and strategies to support communication development.

9. Focus on Strengths and Interests: Identify and leverage the child's strengths and interests to motivate and engage them in communication activities. Incorporate their interests into learning and communication opportunities.

By implementing these strategies at home and in the classroom, parents and teachers can provide effective support for children as they navigate the complex world of communication.

Comorbidity

Comorbidity refers to the co-occurrence of one or more additional medical or psychological conditions alongside autism. This is not uncommon, with research indicating that over 70% of children with autism experience at least one comorbid condition, and nearly 40% grapple with two or more[22]. These comorbid conditions can include attention-deficit/hyperactivity disorder (ADHD), anxiety disorders, learning disabilities, epilepsy, sleep disturbances, and gastrointestinal issues. Each condition adds complexity to the child's life, influencing their development and daily functioning.

Recognizing co-occurring conditions in children with autism brings numerous benefits. Early identification and treatment can significantly improve both physical and mental health, while understanding the full scope of a child's needs allows for more personalized and effective therapeutic strategies. Addressing additional challenges can lead to better developmental outcomes in communication, social skills, and academic performance, as well as a reduction in behavioral issues and improved daily functioning. For families, this means reduced stress and increased support, fostering a more positive home environment. Effective management of co-occurring conditions can also promote greater independence and self-sufficiency in children as they grow. Additionally, awareness of these conditions can lead to access to a broader range of services and supports, ensuring a more holistic approach to care that considers all aspects of a child's well-being. Ultimately, recognizing and addressing co-occurring conditions contributes to a higher quality of life for children with autism and their families.

Compassion

Compassion is the guiding light that illuminates the path of understanding and support, both in the classroom and at home. It's essential for parents and teachers to cultivate this virtue, recognizing that the challenges faced by children with autism are often internal and invisible to the naked eye. Children may struggle to express their wants, needs, or discomforts in ways that others can easily understand, making compassion all the more crucial in navigating their journey.

Parents and teachers must embody compassion in their interactions, understanding that their behaviors may stem from a place of frustration, confusion, or sensory overload. Instead of jumping to conclusions or reacting with frustration, let us pause and approach these situations with empathy and understanding. Behind every outburst or withdrawal may lie a world of unspoken emotions and unmet needs, waiting to be understood and addressed with compassion.

You hold the power to create a safe and nurturing environment where children feel seen, heard, and valued for who they are. This begins with recognizing the internal struggles they may face and the challenges they encounter in navigating a world that often feels overwhelming and unpredictable to them. By extending a hand of compassion, you can bridge the gap between misunderstanding and understanding, fostering trust, connection, and growth in the process. So, let's make compassion our guiding principle in every interaction we have.

Consequences

As for any developing child, it's also okay to enforce consequences. But remember, consequences can be both positive and negative. For example, taking an extra trip to Chick-fil-A because they had a great day at school is a useful consequence in the same way that taking the iPad away for a day could be a reasonable consequence for undesirable behaviors at school. By consistently applying consequences to signify desirable and undesirable behavior, your child can learn the cause-and-effect of their actions.

It's important to understand that withholding consequences for unwanted behavior isn't about being harsh but rather about providing guidance and structure for a child's development. To foster positive behavior, it's vital to implement meaningful consequences. Start by setting clear expectations for behavior, as children, especially those with autism, thrive on routine and predictability. Make the connection between actions and outcomes are clear by choosing consequences that are directly related to the behavior, so that they are relevant and impactful.

NOTES

Data

Data on academic performance and behavior play a crucial role in the education and development of students, especially those with special needs. Collecting and analyzing this data provides a clear and objective picture of a student's progress, strengths, and areas needing improvement.

Academic data helps teachers identify a student's current skill level and track their progress over time. This allows for personalized instruction and support to meet each student's learning needs. Instead of a one-size-fits-all approach, academic data enables a tailored educational experience, ensuring each student receives the support they need to succeed.

Behavior data offers insights into the triggers and patterns of behaviors, helping teachers develop targeted interventions and strategies. Understanding these patterns allows for a more effective response to each student's unique challenges, promoting better behavior management and overall development.

Academic and behavior data form the foundation for evidence-based practices in special education. These practices use research-backed strategies and interventions proven to be effective. Data helps teachers and specialists select and implement the most appropriate interventions based on each student's specific needs and responses. This evidence-based approach increases the likelihood of successful outcomes[23].

Data is essential for monitoring a student's progress over time. Regular assessments and data collection help identify trends, measure growth, and determine whether current interventions are effective. If progress is slower than expected, teachers can adjust strategies and goals accordingly. Without continuous monitoring, it would be challenging to accurately gauge a student's development.

In special education, decisions about a student's educational program, services, and goals must be well-informed and backed by data. Academic and behavior data provide the necessary information to make these decisions effectively. For example, data might reveal that a student requires additional speech therapy or behavioral support, leading to adjustments in their Individualized Education Program (IEP). Data-driven decision-making ensures that resources are allocated where they are most needed.

Data provides a transparent and accountable system for teachers, parents, and administrators. It allows all stakeholders to track a student's progress and ensure they are receiving the appropriate services and support. Data creates a shared understanding of the student's needs.

It's important to ensure that data is collected consistently and accurately. The data collection process for any goal should be well-defined so that if multiple people collected the data, they would all get the same results. This consistency increases the reliability of the data used to more effectively support the student's development.

Now let's break down the different types of data collection methods used when collecting behavior data for students with maladaptive behavior, while explaining what each method entails and when it's most appropriate to use them. Each data collection method has its advantages and is suited to different types of behaviors and situations. Understanding the strengths and limitations of each method can help teachers effectively assess and address maladaptive behaviors in students.

1. Frequency Recording:
Frequency recording involves counting the number of times a specific behavior occurs within a specified period. This method is suitable for behaviors that occur frequently and have clear beginning and ending points. For example, if a student exhibits a behavior like hitting or yelling, frequency recording would involve tallying each instance of the behavior over a set observation period. It's most appropriate for behaviors that occur at a high rate.

2. Duration Recording:
Duration recording involves measuring the length of time a behavior occurs continuously. This method is useful for behaviors that have a clear start and end but may persist for an extended period. For instance, if a student engages in tantrums or self-injurious behaviors, duration recording would involve timing how long each episode lasts. It's most appropriate for behaviors that are prolonged and may disrupt the learning environment.

3. Interval Recording:
Interval recording involves dividing the observation period into intervals and recording whether the behavior occurs during each interval. This method is suitable for behaviors that occur intermittently or are difficult to track continuously. For example, if a student displays off-task behavior in class, interval recording would involve noting whether the behavior occurs within predetermined

intervals, such as every 5 minutes. It's most appropriate for behaviors that fluctuate in frequency or intensity.

4. Time Sampling:
Time sampling involves observing the individual's behavior at specific points in time rather than continuously. This method is useful for gaining a snapshot of behavior patterns over an extended period. For example, if a student exhibits wandering or elopement behavior, time sampling would involve observing the student's location at predetermined intervals throughout the day. It's most appropriate for behaviors that occur sporadically or may be challenging to observe continuously.

5. ABC (Antecedent-Behavior-Consequence) Recording:
ABC recording involves documenting the antecedents (triggers), behaviors, and consequences surrounding a target behavior. This method aims to identify patterns and potential triggers for maladaptive behaviors. For example, if a student engages in aggressive behavior during transitions, ABC recording would involve documenting what happened before (antecedent), the behavior itself, and what happened afterward (consequence). It's most appropriate for understanding the context and function of behaviors.

Remember, no assumptions—data drives decisions! In special education, relying on accurate data helps create the best possible outcomes for each student. Academic and behavior data serve as the compass guiding the educational journey of special needs students. This data informs personalized instruction, facilitates evidence-based practices, monitors progress, enables informed decision-making, ensures accountability, and sets the foundation for meaningful goal setting. Through the careful collection, analysis, and utilization of this data, teachers and specialists can provide the highest quality education and support, helping students achieve their best possible outcomes.

Day Program

A day program for teens and adults with autism is a structured environment designed to provide meaningful activities, skill-building opportunities, and social interaction. These programs aim to enhance the quality of life for participants by promoting personal growth, independence, and a sense of belonging within the community. Day programs offer structured routines, therapeutic interventions, and specialized support tailored to the needs of individuals with autism. Participants engage in various activities suited to their abilities, such as vocational training, life skills development, sensory therapy, and recreational opportunities[24].

To find a suitable day program, parents can start by researching local agencies, schools, or autism-focused organizations. Important factors to consider include the program's reputation, staff qualifications, individualized support plans, and the availability of specialized services like speech therapy or occupational therapy. Visiting the program, observing activities, and speaking with current participants and their families can provide valuable insights. Confirming that the program's philosophy aligns with the family's goals for their child's development and independence is also essential. The key is to find a nurturing and empowering environment that fosters growth and confidence in individuals with autism[25].

Developmental Delay

A developmental delay refers to a condition where a child does not reach developmental milestones typically expected for their age. These milestones cover various aspects of growth, including physical, cognitive, social, and emotional development. Developmental delays can differ in each child but generally involve significant lags in achieving key skills compared to their peers. These delays often become noticeable during early childhood, typically in the first few years of life.

Parents should watch for signs that may indicate a developmental delay. These signs include delays in motor skills like crawling, walking, or talking, as well as difficulty with social interactions, limited communication skills, trouble understanding and following instructions, or persistent behavioral issues. If a child consistently falls behind in multiple areas of development and does not seem to catch up over time, it may raise concerns about a developmental delay.

If parents suspect a developmental delay, the first step is to seek professional evaluation and guidance[26]. This may involve consulting with a pediatrician or a developmental specialist who can conduct assessments and provide a diagnosis if necessary. Early intervention is crucial for addressing developmental delays effectively. Once diagnosed, parents can work closely with healthcare professionals, teachers, and therapists to develop an individualized plan to support their child's development. This plan may include therapies, interventions, and educational strategies tailored to the child's specific needs.

Diet

A healthy diet is a key factor in the overall well-being regardless of their diagnosis with autism. Some children may have sensitivities or allergies to certain foods that can agitate their autism symptoms, while others may benefit from specific dietary interventions. It's important to remember that each child is unique, so what works for one may not work for another[27].

Parents can start by keeping a food diary to track their child's behavior, mood, and physical symptoms after meals. This can help identify patterns and potential food triggers. Common signs of food sensitivities include changes in behavior, gastrointestinal issues, skin problems, and changes in sleep patterns. If you notice consistent negative physical or behavioral reactions to specific foods, consider whether they should be eliminated from your child's diet.

When considering making dietary changes for a child with autism, it's crucial to consult with a healthcare professional or a registered dietitian who specializes in autism and dietary interventions. They can help create a tailored plan that meets your child's nutritional needs while addressing any sensitivities or allergies. Some parents have found success with gluten-free and casein-free (GFCF) diets, while others have explored low-sugar or ketogenic diets. Regardless of the   approach it is important to implement these diets with caution and under professional guidance, as they may not be suitable for all children with autism[28].

Incorporating a variety of nutrient-rich foods, such as fruits, vegetables, lean proteins, and whole grains, can be beneficial for overall health. Additionally, some children may benefit from supplements like omega-3 fatty acids or probiotics, but these should also be discussed with a healthcare provider.

Discrete Trial Training (DTT)

Discrete Trial Training (DTT) is a structured and systematic teaching method commonly used in Applied Behavior Analysis (ABA) therapy for individuals with autism and other developmental disorders. It is a teaching approach that breaks down complex skills or behaviors into smaller, discrete components or trials, hence the name "discrete trial."[29] Each trial consists of three main components:

1. Antecedent or Instruction: This is the prompt or instruction given to the individual, specifying what behavior is expected. For example, if the goal is to teach a child to say "apple" when shown an apple, the antecedent could be the question, "What is this?"

2. Response: This is the individual's behavioral response to the instruction. In the example above, the response would be the child saying "apple."

3. Consequence or Feedback: The consequence is the outcome that follows the individual's response. In DTT, positive reinforcement is often used as a consequence. If the child correctly says "apple," they may receive praise or a small reward as positive reinforcement.

The primary goal of DTT is to teach and reinforce specific, target behaviors or skills. It is highly structured and typically involves intensive one-on-one teaching sessions with a trained therapist or instructor. DTT can be used to teach a wide range of skills, including communication, social, self-help, and academic skills. The structured nature of DTT allows for precise data collection and measurement of a child's progress, making it a valuable tool. It is often used as part of a comprehensive treatment plan to address the individualized needs of children with autism and other developmental challenges.

Parents and teachers both hold significant roles in utilizing Discrete Trial Training (DTT) to support children with autism spectrum disorder (ASD), whether at home or in the classroom. While DTT is commonly administered by trained therapists in clinical or educational settings, parents and teachers can incorporate its principles into their respective environments to foster structured learning opportunities. Here's how parents can implement DTT at home and what teachers can do in the classroom:

For Parents:

1. Identify Target Skills: Pinpoint specific skills or behaviors you aim to teach your child, such as communication, social interaction, self-help, or academic concepts.

2. Break Skills Down: Divide the target skill into smaller, manageable steps to facilitate learning and mastery.

3. Create a Structured Environment: Establish a quiet, well-lit area at home conducive to focused learning, minimizing distractions.

4. Provide Clear Instructions: Offer simple, consistent instructions supported by visual aids to enhance understanding.

5. Use Prompts: Initially provide prompts or cues to assist your child's responses, gradually reducing them as proficiency improves.

6. Reinforcement: Employ positive reinforcement, such as praise or rewards, to motivate and reinforce desired behaviors.

7. Repetition and Practice: Practice each step of the skill repeatedly to build fluency and independence.

8. Data Collection: Keep records of your child's progress to track improvement and adjust teaching strategies accordingly.

9. Be Patient and Flexible: Understand that progress may vary and be patient and adaptable in your approach.

10. Generalization: Encourage your child to apply newly acquired skills in different settings and situations for broader applicability.

11. Seek Professional Guidance: Consult with trained therapists or behavior analysts to develop a comprehensive treatment plan tailored to your child's needs.

For Teachers:

1. Incorporate DTT into Lessons: Integrate DTT principles into classroom activities and lessons, aligning them with individualized education plans (IEPs) and goals.

2. Provide Structured Learning Opportunities: Designate specific times for DTT sessions within the classroom schedule, ensuring a structured and supportive environment.

3. Offer Clear Instructions: Deliver instructions in a concise, consistent manner, supplementing verbal cues with visual aids as needed.

4. Utilize Reinforcement: Use positive reinforcement techniques to encourage and motivate students' participation and progress.

5. Individualize Instruction: Tailor DTT sessions to each student's needs and abilities, adjusting prompts and pacing accordingly.

6. Collaborate with Support Staff: Work closely with special education staff, therapists, and support personnel to coordinate DTT implementation and monitor progress.

7. Monitor and Assess Progress: Regularly evaluate students' responses and progress during DTT sessions, making data-driven decisions to refine teaching strategies.

By implementing DTT effectively at home and in the classroom, parents and teachers can support the development and growth of children with autism, fostering meaningful progress and success in various domains of functioning.

Dyspraxia

Dyspraxia, also known as Developmental Coordination Disorder (DCD), is a neurodevelopmental disorder that primarily affects a person's ability to plan and coordinate physical movements. This condition can impact both fine motor skills, which involve precise hand-eye coordination, and gross motor skills, which encompass activities like running or jumping. While dyspraxia is not limited to children with autism, it can co-occur with autism[30].

Children with dyspraxia often struggle with tasks that require intricate hand-eye coordination, such as writing, drawing, buttoning shirts, or tying shoelaces. They may find it difficult to hold and use tools like pencils or scissors effectively, which can affect their academic performance and daily activities. Dyspraxia can also affect gross motor skills, making it challenging for children to engage in physical activities that involve coordination, such as riding a bike, catching a ball, or participating in organized sports. Their movements may appear clumsy or uncoordinated, leading to potential difficulties in sports and recreational activities.

Many children with dyspraxia may also experience sensory sensitivities. These sensitivities can affect their ability to engage in activities that involve sensory input, such as touch, texture, or movement. Sensory sensitivities can add an extra layer of complexity to their daily experiences.

Individualized support and accommodations can make a significant difference in helping children with dyspraxia overcome motor skill challenges and thrive in various aspects of life. Creating a supportive environment that acknowledges their strengths and provides the necessary tools and strategies to navigate their daily activities successfully is key to their well-being and development.

NOTES

Early Intervention

Early intervention in autism is a pivotal step that can make a profound difference in a child's developmental trajectory and overall quality of life. Extensive research and statistics consistently underscore the incredible benefits of intervening early when a child is suspected to have autism. These benefits span across various aspects of a child's growth and development.

One of the most significant advantages of early intervention is the noticeable improvement in developmental outcomes. Children who receive early intervention services often exhibit substantial progress in their communication skills, social interactions, behavior, and overall development. This early support helps bridge the developmental gaps that children with autism may face and sets a strong foundation for their future growth.

Early intervention equips children with autism with essential skills that enhance their readiness for school. These skills encompass effective communication, cooperation with peers, and emotional regulation, all of which are crucial for academic success and positive social interactions within a school environment. Early intervention empowers these children to enter school with a greater level of preparedness, setting them up for a more successful educational journey.

A compelling factor in favor of early intervention is its long-term cost-effectiveness. While the initial investment in early intervention services may seem significant, it often leads to substantial savings over the child's lifetime[31]. This is because early intervention helps children acquire vital skills and may reduce the need for extensive special education and support services in the future. The cost savings, in addition to the positive impact on the child's life, make early intervention a wise investment.

Furthermore, early intervention focuses on increasing a child's independence. By addressing developmental delays and providing targeted support at an early age, children with autism can develop the skills necessary for greater self-reliance. This independence benefits both the child and their parents

For parents who suspect their child may need help, several crucial steps should be taken. Trusting your parental instincts is paramount; if you notice any signs of developmental delays or autism, seek a professional evaluation. A pediatrician or developmental specialist can provide a comprehensive assessment and diagnosis. Accessing early intervention services as soon as possible is vital. These services may include speech therapy, occupational therapy, behavioral therapy, and specialized educational programs tailored to your child's needs.

Active participation in your child's early intervention journey is key. Collaborate closely with therapists and teachers, set achievable goals, and engage in home-based activities to reinforce their progress. It's also beneficial to connect with support networks, such as local autism organizations and parent support groups. These networks can offer guidance, emotional support, and valuable insights from families who have gone through similar experiences.

Echolalia

Echolalia is a language phenomenon characterized by the repetition of words, phrases, or sentences spoken by others. In children with autism, echolalia often manifests as the immediate or delayed repetition of words or phrases heard from others, from TV shows, or from their own previous utterances. It's a common communication trait observed in many individuals on the autism spectrum[32].

Echolalia serves various functions for children with autism, including communication, self-soothing, and language acquisition. While it may seem repetitive or unusual to outsiders, it can actually be a form of communication for the child, as they use familiar phrases to convey their needs, express emotions, or make sense of their surroundings. However, it can also pose challenges in social interactions and language development if not addressed appropriately[33].

Parents and teachers can address echolalia in children with understanding and targeted interventions:

1. Understanding the Function: Recognizing the underlying function of echolalia is crucial. Parents and teachers should observe when and why the child engages in echolalia to understand its communicative purpose. This understanding can guide appropriate responses and interventions.

2. Communication Training: Provide alternative communication strategies and teach functional language skills to help the child express their needs and desires more effectively. This may include teaching specific phrases or using visual supports to aid communication.

3. Responding Positively: Responding positively to echolalia can encourage communication and language development. Acknowledge the child's attempts to communicate, even if it involves echolalia, and respond appropriately to the intended meaning behind their repetition.

4. Modeling and Expansion: Model correct language use and expand on the child's echolalic utterances to provide meaningful language input. For example, if a child repeats "Want juice," respond with, "Yes, you want juice. Let's go get some juice."

5. Promoting Turn-Taking: Encourage interactive communication by promoting turn-taking in conversations. Use structured activities and social scripts to teach the child the appropriate times to speak and listen in a conversation.

6. Functional Communication Training: Implement functional communication training to teach the child alternative ways to express their needs and desires. This may involve teaching specific phrases or using visual supports to aid communication.

7. Visual Supports: Utilize visual supports, such as picture cards or communication boards, to help the child express themselves and understand language in context. Visual supports can provide concrete representations of language concepts and support comprehension.

8. Reinforcement: Provide positive reinforcement for using appropriate communication strategies and reducing echolalic speech. Celebrate the child's progress and efforts in developing functional communication skills.

By addressing echolalia with understanding, targeted interventions, and supportive strategies, parents and teachers can help children with autism develop more effective communication skills and navigate social interactions more successfully. It's essential to approach echolalia with patience, empathy, and a focus on promoting the child's overall communication and language development.

Eligibility

An Individualized Education Program (IEP) eligibility is a crucial process that determines whether a student qualifies for specialized educational support. Think of it as the key to unlocking personalized assistance for students with disabilities. Unlike a formal diagnosis, IEP eligibility focuses on assessing a student's educational needs rather than confirming a specific medical or clinical condition. A team consisting of teachers, specialists, and parents evaluates the student's academic performance and potential barriers to learning. If they find that the student's learning is significantly affected, the student becomes eligible for an IEP, a tailor-made plan designed to address their learning requirements[34].

It's important to distinguish IEP eligibility from a formal diagnosis. While a formal diagnosis confirms a specific condition or disability through medical or clinical means, it doesn't automatically grant eligibility for an IEP. The critical factor is whether the diagnosed condition substantially impacts the student's learning and necessitates special education services. For instance, a student might have a formal diagnosis like Attention Deficit Hyperactivity Disorder (ADHD) but perform well academically, not requiring specialized educational support. In such cases, the diagnosis exists, but IEP eligibility might not apply[35]. In essence, IEP eligibility acts as a bridge connecting a student's learning needs to tailored educational assistance, ensuring that every student, regardless of their challenges, has the opportunity to excel in their academic journey.

Elopement

Elopement refers to the behavior where a child leaves a supervised or safe environment without the knowledge or consent of their caregivers. This behavior is sometimes also referred to as "wandering" or "bolting." Elopement can pose significant challenges and risks for children with autism and their families. According to a study published in the *Journal of Child Psychology and Psychiatry* nearly half of children with autism engage in elopement behaviors at some point during childhood[36]. This behavior tends to be more common in children with autism compared to their typically developing peers.

Elopement can be extremely dangerous. Children may wander into potentially hazardous situations, such as traffic, bodies of water, or unfamiliar areas, which can result in accidents or injuries. Statistics show that wandering-related incidents are one of the leading causes of injury and mortality among children with autism. Additionally, elopement can cause immense stress and anxiety for parents and caregivers who fear for their child's safety.

Elopement can have various triggers, including sensory sensitivities, the desire for exploration, seeking preferred activities or objects, or escaping from overwhelming or aversive situations. It's essential to understand that elopement is often not a deliberate act of defiance but a response to internal or external stimuli. Here are some tips to help keep children safe from elopement:

1.   Environment Modification: Parents can make their home environment safer by installing locks on doors and windows that the child cannot easily open. Additionally, using alarms or chimes on doors can alert caregivers when a child attempts to leave.

2. Identification: Children can wear identification, such as an ID bracelet or a card with contact information, in case they do wander and become separated from caregivers.

3.   Communication and Education: Teach the child safety rules and boundaries, including not leaving the house without permission and not approaching strangers. Use visual supports and social stories to reinforce these lessons.

4. Tracking Devices: GPS tracking devices designed for children can be worn discreetly and provide real-time location information to caregivers. These devices can be a valuable tool in keeping track of a child's whereabouts.

5. Community Support: Inform neighbors, school staff, and local law enforcement about a child's elopement tendencies. Building a support network can help prepare those in your community to respond quickly in case of elopement.

Teachers play a critical role in helping their students with autism refrain from eloping by implementing proactive strategies and creating a supportive learning environment:

1.   Understanding Triggers: Teachers should strive to understand the individual triggers that may prompt elopement in their students with autism. This may involve conducting functional behavior assessments to identify specific antecedents and environmental factors that contribute to elopement behaviors.

2.   Individualized Supports: Implement individualized supports and accommodations to address the needs of each student. This may include sensory accommodations, such as providing sensory breaks or creating calming sensory spaces within the classroom, to help students regulate their sensory experiences and reduce the likelihood of elopement.

3.   Structured Environment: Create a structured and predictable learning environment that minimizes unexpected changes or disruptions. Establish consistent routines and visual schedules to help students with autism feel more secure and less likely to elope in response to unfamiliar or chaotic situations.

4.   Supervision and Monitoring: Maintain close supervision and monitoring of students with autism, particularly those who are at higher risk of elopement. Do your best to ensure that there is always adult supervision during transitions, outdoor activities, and other potentially risky situations.

5. Social Stories and Visual Supports: Use social stories and visual supports to teach students about appropriate behaviors and safety rules related to elopement. Create personalized social stories that address the consequences of elopement and teach alternative coping strategies for managing overwhelming situations.

6. Functional Communication Training: Teach students alternative ways to communicate their needs and desires effectively. Provide communication tools and strategies, such as picture exchange communication systems (PECS) or communication apps, to help students express themselves and request assistance when needed, reducing the likelihood of elopement as a means of communication.

7. Positive Reinforcement: Use positive reinforcement to encourage and reward appropriate behaviors and adherence to safety rules. Reinforce students for following directions, staying within designated areas, and seeking assistance from adults when feeling overwhelmed or distressed.

By implementing these proactive strategies and creating a supportive learning environment, teachers can help their students with autism refrain from elopement and provide safe and well suited educational settings. It's essential to approach elopement with empathy, understanding, and a commitment to providing individualized support that meets the needs of each student.

Emotional Regulation

Emotional regulation is a crucial skill for children's social and emotional development. It refers to the ability to recognize, understand, and manage emotions effectively, including expressing them appropriately, coping with stress, and adapting to changing situations. Children with autism often face challenges in emotional regulation due to the characteristics of the diagnosis. They may struggle with identifying and labeling their own emotions or understanding others', leading to difficulties in social interactions. Additionally, sensory sensitivities can trigger strong emotional responses, requiring children to learn to manage and cope with these sensory challenges[37].

Developing emotional regulation skills is essential for several reasons. It contributes to improved social interactions, helping them engage positively with peers and communicate their feelings effectively. It also aids in managing anxiety and stress, empowering children to cope with overwhelming situations and reducing the impact of stressors. Furthermore, emotional regulation is linked to behavior management, as children who struggle to regulate their emotions may exhibit challenging behaviors. Teaching emotional regulation skills can help reduce these behaviors and promote more adaptive responses.

For parents, supporting their child's emotional regulation involves creating a structured environment that minimizes sensory triggers when possible. Teaching emotional vocabulary and using visual supports can help children identify and express their feelings. Techniques such as deep breathing exercises and mindfulness can also be valuable tools for managing emotional responses. Teachers can also promote emotional regulation by creating a supportive classroom environment, providing sensory accommodations, and teaching coping strategies to help children regulate their emotions effectively. By working together, parents and teachers can help children with autism develop essential emotional regulation skills to navigate social interactions and manage their emotions more effectively.

Executive Functioning

Executive functioning refers to a set of cognitive processes and skills responsible for managing and controlling various aspects of daily life. It plays a crucial role in organizing thoughts, planning and executing tasks, managing time, regulating emotions, and adapting to changing situations. These functions are vital for success in academics, social interactions, and everyday activities. When it comes to children with autism, executive functioning can be an area of particular importance and challenge[38].

Children with autism often exhibit a range of executive functioning difficulties, although the extent varies from one individual to another. Common executive functioning challenges include difficulties with organization and planning. Children may struggle to create structured routines, plan tasks, or initiate and complete multi-step activities. For example, they may find it challenging to organize their school materials or plan out the steps needed to complete a homework assignment[39].

Additionally, they may face challenges in managing their time effectively and have difficulty estimating the time needed for tasks or adhering to schedules and deadlines. This can impact their academic performance and daily routines, leading to frustration and stress. Emotional regulation is another aspect of executive functioning that can be affected. Children with autism may experience difficulty in identifying and managing their own emotions and understanding the emotions of others. This can lead to challenges in social interactions, as they may struggle to respond appropriately to others' emotional cues or regulate their own emotional responses.

Flexibility and adaptability, key components of executive functioning, can also pose challenges. Children with autism may have a preference for routines and sameness, making it challenging to adapt to unexpected changes or transitions. This rigidity can impact their ability to navigate novel situations and cope with unexpected events.

Problem-solving and decision-making skills are integral parts of executive functioning as well. Some children may have difficulty evaluating options, considering consequences, and making informed choices. This can affect their ability to make decisions independently and solve problems effectively. However, it's important to note that executive functioning challenges in children with autism are not uniform. Some children may excel in certain aspects of executive functioning while facing difficulties in others. Additionally, with appropriate support and interventions, many children with autism can develop and improve their executive functioning skills over time[40].

Recognizing these challenges and providing tailored interventions and strategies is essential for helping children thrive. Teachers, therapists, and parents can work together to create structured environments, implement visual supports, teach self-regulation techniques, and develop individualized strategies to support the child's executive functioning needs. By addressing these challenges proactively, children can enhance their ability to navigate daily life successfully and achieve their fullest potential.

Expectations

"No one rises to low expectations." - Les Brown

It's a beautiful thing when parents and teachers hold both realistic and high expectations for children with autism. This approach acknowledges the abilities and challenges of each child while also recognizing their immense potential for growth and development. By setting realistic goals that are attainable yet still challenging, we create a supportive environment where children can thrive and reach their full potential.

One of the pitfalls of having low expectations is that it can inadvertently limit a child's progress and hinder their development. When we underestimate a child's abilities or potential, we may unintentionally communicate to them that we don't believe they are capable of achieving more. This can lead to feelings of frustration, low self-esteem, and missed opportunities for growth.

Seeing beyond the surface is crucial when it comes to supporting children with autism. Instead of focusing solely on their current abilities or challenges, we must adopt the mindset that "nobody rises to low expectations." This means believing in the child's potential and refusing to settle for anything less than their best. By holding high expectations, we challenge children to push beyond their comfort zones, explore new possibilities, and unlock hidden talents and abilities they may not even know they possess.

Parents and teachers have the incredible opportunity to be change agents in the lives of children with autism. By embracing a mindset of high expectations and unwavering belief in the child's potential, we can inspire them to dream big, work hard, and achieve greatness. Together, we can create a world where every child, regardless of their abilities or challenges, is empowered to reach their full potential and shine brightly in their own way.

Exposure

Exposing children with autism to the same experiences as their neurotypical peers is essential for their growth and development. It promotes learning, social integration, skill development, and broadens their horizons. Even more crucial is the importance of trying. We may never truly know how much children are downloading from their environment so why not provide opportunities for them to soak up information they may not be exposed to otherwise. Sometimes it's enough to be "in the room where it happens"!

Here are some things parents can do to directly and indirectly provide opportunities for exposure:

1. Audiobooks and Podcasts: Introduce them to audiobooks and educational podcasts that cover a wide range of topics. These mediums offer engaging content and can enhance listening and comprehension skills.

2. Hands-On Activities: Engage in hands-on activities related to advanced topics. For instance, if exploring space, create a model of the solar system or conduct simple science experiments. Provide as much assistance required to physically include them in the activity.

3. Inclusive Social Activities: Encourage participation in inclusive social activities where they can interact with neurotypical peers who may introduce them to new

interests and knowledge. This could include recreational sports or other hobbies.

4. Family Outings: Plan family outings to museums, science centers, and cultural events. These experiences expose them to a wide range of subjects in an interactive and engaging manner.

5. Educational TV and Documentaries: Select educational TV shows and documentaries that align with their interests. These programs often simplify complex subjects and make learning enjoyable.

Teachers can take various steps to expose students with autism to the same experiences as their neurotypical peers, fostering inclusion and supporting their overall development:

1. Inclusive Curriculum: Ensure that the curriculum is inclusive and accessible to all students, including those with autism. Provide materials in different formats and incorporate visual aids to accommodate diverse learning styles.

2. Differentiated Instruction: Tailor instruction to meet the individual needs of students with autism. Use a variety of teaching strategies, such as hands-on activities, visual supports, and multi-sensory approaches, to engage students and facilitate learning.

3. Peer Interaction: Facilitate opportunities for students with autism to interact with their neurotypical peers in inclusive settings. Encourage collaboration on group

projects, pair students for activities, and promote social interaction during classroom discussions and activities.

4. Sensory Supports: Create a sensory-friendly classroom environment that accommodates the sensory needs of students with autism. Provide quiet areas for relaxation, use visual schedules to promote predictability, and minimize sensory distractions to support focus and attention.

5. Structured Routines: Establish structured routines and clear expectations to help students with autism navigate the school day more effectively. Use visual schedules, task lists, and verbal prompts to guide students through daily activities and transitions.

6. Social Skills Instruction: Incorporate social skills instruction into the curriculum to help students with autism develop social competence and navigate social interactions. Teach skills such as turn-taking, perspective-taking, and conflict resolution through role-playing, modeling, and explicit instruction.

7. Positive Reinforcement: Use positive reinforcement to motivate and encourage students with autism. Recognize and celebrate their achievements, no matter how small, to build confidence and self-esteem.

8. Collaboration with Support Staff: Collaborate with special education teachers, speech therapists, and other support staff to provide targeted interventions and accommodations for students with autism. Work together to develop individualized education plans (IEPs) and implement strategies to address specific needs.

9. Parent Involvement: Involve parents in their child's education by keeping them informed about classroom activities, progress, and challenges. Solicit input from parents regarding their child's strengths, preferences, and goals to inform instructional planning.

10. Professional Development: Seek out professional development opportunities to enhance knowledge and skills related to supporting students with autism. Attend workshops, conferences, and trainings to stay informed about best practices and evidence-based strategies.

By implementing these strategies, teachers can create inclusive learning environments that promote the full participation and academic success of students with autism alongside their neurotypical peers.

Expressive Language

Expressive language refers to the ability to communicate thoughts, ideas, and feelings effectively using words, gestures, or other forms of communication. It involves producing spoken or written language, as well as nonverbal communication such as facial expressions, body language, and gestures. Expressive language skills typically develop gradually, starting with babbling in infancy and progressing to complex sentences as children grow[41].

For children with autism, expressive language development may be delayed or impaired. They may have difficulty using words to express their thoughts, forming grammatically correct sentences, or relying on nonverbal communication methods.

Both parents and teachers play a crucial role in supporting the development of expressive language skills in children with autism. It is imperative to create a communication-rich environment from the beginning. This means providing plenty of opportunities for meaningful conversations and interactions. Parents and teachers can engage in conversations with the child on various topics, ask open-ended questions, and actively listen to what the child has to say. By encouraging communication and showing that their thoughts are valued, adults can stimulate the child's expressive language development[42].

Modeling correct language use is also essential. Children often learn by imitating, so parents and teachers can serve as language models. Speaking clearly, using proper grammar, and expanding on what the child says can help them understand how language works. When the child communicates, adults can respond by repeating their statements and adding more details, showing them how to use language effectively.

Using visual supports, such as picture cards or communication boards, can be incredibly helpful for children with autism. These visual aids provide a way for the child to communicate when verbal expression is difficult. Parents and teachers can work with the child to use these tools to express their needs and desires effectively, bridging the gap between their thoughts and communication[43].

Encouraging the child to initiate conversations is another valuable strategy. Parents and teachers can show genuine interest in the child's interests and activities, prompting them to start conversations. By asking questions related to their hobbies or preferences, adults provide opportunities for the child to take the lead in communication, which can help improve their expressive language skills.

Additionally, providing choices can empower the child and support their communication development. Giving them options in everyday situations encourages decision-making and the expression of preferences. For example, offering choices like "Do you want juice or water?" allows the child to make decisions and express their desires, which can strengthen their communication abilities.

These strategies, when implemented with patience and empathy, can make a significant difference in a child's expressive language development. By working together, parents and teachers can support children with autism in effectively expressing themselves and engaging in meaningful communication.

NOTES

504 Plan

A 504 plan is a customized accommodation plan designed to ensure that students with disabilities have equitable access to education and all school-related activities. It gets its name from Section 504 of the Rehabilitation Act of 1973, a federal law that prohibits discrimination based on disability in any program receiving federal funding, including public schools. These plans are crucial tools in providing students with disabilities the support and accommodations they need to excel in an educational environment.

Determining if a child requires a 504 plan involves recognizing situations where such a plan might be necessary. Generally, a 504 plan is considered when a student has a disability that significantly impacts one or more major life activities. Disabilities can include physical conditions like diabetes, mental health disorders like anxiety, learning disabilities, ADHD, or other health impairments. The key factor is whether the disability substantially limits the student's ability to engage in educational activities.

If there is a suspicion that a child may need a 504 plan, the first step is to communicate with the school staff. The school will then initiate an evaluation process to assess the child's needs. This evaluation typically involves gathering information from various sources, including teachers, healthcare professionals, and parents. For a child to qualify for a 504 plan, there must be documented evidence of a disability that significantly impedes their ability to access and benefit from their education[44]. This documentation may include medical reports, assessments, or evaluations conducted by qualified professionals.

Once a 504 plan is established, it undergoes periodic reviews to ensure it continues to meet the child's evolving needs. Adjustments are made as necessary based on the child's progress and changing circumstances to ensure they receive the most effective support. The ultimate goal is to provide a conducive learning environment where a child can thrive despite their disability, promoting equal access to education for all students.

Faith

Navigating the journey of raising and teaching children with autism requires faith. Having faith doesn't mean having all the answers or knowing exactly what the future holds. Instead, it means believing in each child's potential and possibilities, regardless of the challenges they face. It involves trusting in their innate ability to learn, grow, and shine brightly, even in adversity.

Faith empowers us to see beyond the limitations and barriers that autism may present. It encourages us to focus on the boundless potential within each child. Every small milestone achieved is a triumph to be celebrated, reflecting the unwavering determination and resilience of both the child and their supporters. In moments of doubt or uncertainty, let faith guide you, filling your efforts with hope and determination.

Faith becomes a beacon of hope, gently illuminating the darkest days. It instills resilience, teaching us to embrace every moment with trust that there is beauty in each step forward, no matter how small it may seem. With faith, we find inner strength we never knew we possessed. This strength helps us navigate the complexities of therapies, educational decisions, and advocacy with grace and determination. Faith reminds us that we are never alone on this journey, even in moments of isolation.

Finding communities of like-minded individuals who share similar experiences can be tremendously helpful in building and maintaining faith. Sharing stories and receiving encouragement from other parents and teachers who understand is incredibly valuable. These communities offer shared wisdom and comfort, reinforcing the belief that, together, we can overcome any challenge.

FAPE (Free Appropriate Public Education)

FAPE stands for Free Appropriate Public Education, which is a legal right guaranteed to all students under the Individuals with Disabilities Education Act (IDEA). FAPE ensures that children with disabilities, including those with autism, have access to a public education that meets their unique needs at no cost to their families. It is designed to provide students with the necessary supports and services to enable them to make progress in their educational goals and participate fully in school activities[45].

FAPE helps students with disabilities by making provisions so they receive an education tailored to their individual needs. This may include specialized instruction, accommodations, modifications, related services (such as speech therapy or occupational therapy), assistive technology, and other supports as outlined in their Individualized Education Program (IEP) or 504 plan. By providing these services, FAPE aims to level the playing field for students with disabilities and promote their academic and social development.

Parents play a crucial role in ensuring that FAPE is being granted to their child. They can advocate for their child's educational rights by actively participating in the Individualized Education Program (IEP) or 504 plan process, attending meetings, and collaborating with school staff to develop appropriate goals and supports. Parents can also stay informed about their child's progress and educational rights under IDEA, and if necessary, seek support from advocacy organizations or legal resources to facilitate their child receiving the services they are entitled to.

Teachers have a responsibility to uphold FAPE by providing a supportive and inclusive learning environment that meets the diverse needs of all students, including those with disabilities. They can do this by implementing evidence-based instructional strategies, accommodations, and modifications outlined in students' IEPs or 504 plans. Teachers should collaborate with special education staff and related service providers to address students' individual needs and monitor their progress towards academic and functional goals. Additionally, teachers should maintain open communication with parents and actively involve them in their child's educational program to ensure that FAPE is being implemented effectively.

In summary, FAPE is a legal right that ensures students with disabilities have access to an education that meets their individual needs. Parents can advocate for FAPE by actively participating in the educational planning process, while teachers can uphold FAPE by providing a supportive and inclusive learning environment that addresses students' unique needs. By working together, parents and teachers can help support students with disabilities so they receive the services and accommodations they need to succeed in school and beyond.

FERPA (Family Educational Rights and Privacy Act)

FERPA, or the Family Educational Rights and Privacy Act, is a federal law designed to safeguard the confidentiality of student education records. It grants specific rights to parents and eligible students concerning these records. The act sets forth guidelines that schools and educational institutions must follow to ensure that student information remains private and is only disclosed under designated conditions. This balance between maintaining privacy and facilitating necessary information sharing is a key aspect of FERPA's purpose.

Rights Under FERPA

1. Access to Records: Parents and eligible students (those who are 18 years old or older, or who attend a postsecondary institution) have the right to access and review their educational records. This includes the right to inspect and copy records maintained by the school.

2. Request to Amend Records: Parents and eligible students can request changes to educational records if they believe the information is inaccurate, misleading, or in violation of privacy rights. Schools must consider these requests and may be required to amend records if the request is deemed valid.

3. Consent for Disclosure: Schools must obtain written consent from parents or eligible students before disclosing personally identifiable information from educational records, except in certain circumstances. FERPA outlines specific situations where disclosure is permitted without consent, such as to school officials with a legitimate

educational interest, in response to a judicial order, or in connection with health and safety emergencies.

4. Annual Notification: Schools are required to notify parents and eligible students annually about their FERPA rights. This notification typically includes information on how to access records, how to request amendments, and how to file complaints regarding violations of FERPA.

Educational institutions must implement policies and procedures to comply with FERPA, including training staff on privacy practices, maintaining secure record-keeping systems, and handling record requests according to the law. FERPA itself is designed to protect student privacy by regulating access to and sharing of educational records. It grants parents and eligible students the rights to access, amend, and control the disclosure of these records. Schools must adhere to FERPA regulations to ensure both the protection of student privacy and transparency in compliance.

First/Then

A First/Then board is a visual support tool designed to help children with autism and other developmental or communication challenges understand and complete tasks or activities. Its primary purpose is to provide a clear and structured way to communicate expectations and transitions, making daily routines and activities more manageable and less stressful.

One key benefit of a First/Then board is that it offers a visual representation of what a child needs to do. For children with autism, who often process information more effectively through visual cues, this is invaluable. It provides a concrete way to convey the sequence of activities or tasks. The "First" part of the board shows the initial task or activity that needs to be completed, while the "Then" part shows what comes next. This visual clarity helps children better understand the order of events and what is expected of them.

The First/Then board introduces predictability by showing children exactly what will happen next. This can reduce anxiety and uncertainty, as the child knows what to expect. It can be especially beneficial during transitions or when introducing a change in routine. By providing a clear visual sequence, the board helps the child mentally prepare for what is to come, promoting smoother transitions between activities.

Another significant advantage of the First/Then board is its capacity to motivate and reinforce positive behavior. The "Then" part often features a preferred activity or reward. This serves as an incentive for the child to complete the initial task. It taps into the child's intrinsic motivation and provides a tangible goal to work towards. For example, if the "First" task is completing homework, the "Then" reward could be playing with a favorite toy. This positive reinforcement encourages the child to stay on task and complete the required activity.

Children with autism may face challenges in expressing their needs or understanding verbal instructions. The visual nature of the First/Then board bypasses some of these communication hurdles. It offers a non-verbal means of conveying expectations and transitions, reducing frustration for both the child and caregivers. Additionally, it can be customized with images or symbols that are meaningful to the child, making it more personalized and effective.

Overall, the First/Then board serves as a powerful tool in supporting children with autism by providing visual clarity, predictability, motivation, and a means to reduce communication challenges. Its purpose is to create a structured and supportive environment that helps these children navigate daily routines and activities with greater ease, reducing anxiety and promoting positive behavior and learning.

Fixations

Fixation in the context of autism refers to a strong and persistent focus on a specific topic, object, or activity. These fixations can be intense and all-consuming for the child. They may manifest as a deep fascination with a particular subject, repetitive behaviors, or a strong attachment to a specific object or routine. Fixations are common in autism and often serve as a coping mechanism or source of comfort for children on the spectrum[46].

The effects of fixation can vary but typically include intense engagement with the chosen focus. Children may become deeply engrossed in their fixation, displaying heightened interest and attention. However, fixations can also lead to reduced flexibility in routines and activities, making it challenging for children to adapt to changes or disruptions. Communication may be affected as children may prefer to focus solely on their fixation, potentially limiting their interaction with others. This can sometimes result in social isolation.

Understanding why a child has a fixation can be very beneficial to parents and teachers. Recognizing that fixations often serve as coping mechanisms is crucial. Balancing acceptance and encouragement is necessary, as gently encouraging children to engage in a variety of activities can promote a broader range of interests and skills. Some fixations can be educational, so parents and teachers can explore opportunities for learning within the context of the fixation.

Additionally, the fixation can be used as a tool for teaching and skill development. Encouraging social interaction related to the fixation, such as arranging playdates with peers who share the interest, can foster social skill development. Gradually introducing new interests alongside the fixation can help children become more flexible in their interests and routines. Seeking professional guidance may be necessary if the fixation is causing significant disruption or interference with the child's development. Ultimately, creating a supportive environment that accommodates the fixation while gently guiding the child to explore new interests can help them navigate their fixations in a healthy and constructive manner.

Food Aversions and Sensitivities

Food sensitivities have gained attention in recent years, especially concerning individuals on the autism spectrum. While food sensitivities are different from food allergies, they can significantly impact a person's physical and behavioral well-being. Food sensitivities refer to adverse reactions to certain foods or components of foods, which may not be as immediate or severe as allergies but can still cause discomfort. Understanding and addressing these challenges are essential to support the dietary needs of children with autism.

Many individuals with autism may experience gastrointestinal issues, such as constipation, diarrhea, or abdominal pain, associated with specific food sensitivities.

These gastrointestinal problems can exacerbate some of the behavioral challenges often seen in individuals with autism. Discomfort or pain related to food sensitivities can contribute to irritability, anxiety, and other behavioral issues[47].

Identifying specific food triggers can be challenging as sensitivities can vary widely among individuals. Common culprits include gluten, dairy, artificial additives, and certain proteins. The process of identifying these triggers often involves meticulous observation, elimination diets, and consultation with healthcare professionals.

Children with autism often have heightened sensory sensitivities, including those related to taste, texture, smell, and even the visual appearance of food. These sensitivities can lead to aversions to certain foods, making mealtime a challenging experience. For example, a child may have an aversion to foods with specific textures, such as mushy or slimy textures, and may refuse to eat them. Even the taste of the same food, like blueberries, can vary, leading to different reactions.

Addressing food aversions in children with autism due to sensory issues is crucial for supporting their nutritional needs and overall well-being. Parents can help children expand their food preferences by gradually introducing new foods and creating a positive mealtime environment. Managing food sensitivities in individuals with autism is essential for promoting better physical and behavioral health. The relationship between food sensitivities and autism is complex and varies from person to person, making careful observation, consultation with healthcare professionals, and tailored dietary modifications key steps in addressing these sensitivities effectively.

Functional Behavior Analysis (FBA)

A Functional Behavior Assessment (FBA) is a systematic process used to understand and analyze challenging behaviors displayed by children, particularly those with developmental or behavioral issues such as autism or emotional disorders. The primary purpose of an FBA is to identify the underlying causes or functions of these behaviors. By understanding why a child exhibits certain challenging behaviors, professionals and caregivers can develop effective strategies to address and manage these behaviors more appropriately.

A child typically undergoes an FBA when they consistently exhibit challenging behaviors that significantly interfere with their ability to learn, socialize, or engage in daily activities. These behaviors might include aggression, self-injury, non-compliance, or disruptive conduct. An FBA is often initiated when parents, teachers, or school professionals recognize the need to better understand and address these behaviors to create a more conducive learning and social environment for the child[6].

A child may require an FBA for several reasons. One reason is that it helps uncover the root causes or functions of the challenging behaviors. Second, it facilitates the development of targeted and individualized intervention strategies tailored to the child's specific needs. An FBA also helps create a supportive and personalized Behavior Intervention Plan (BIP) that aims to reduce the occurrence of challenging behaviors and replace them with more appropriate alternatives. Overall, the goal is to improve the child's overall well-being, learning experience, and social interactions.

Creating an FBA is a collaborative effort involving a team of professionals with expertise in areas such as special education, behavior analysis, school psychology, and, in some cases, speech or occupational therapy. This interdisciplinary team works together to collect data, conduct assessments, analyze behavior patterns, and determine the functions or reasons behind the challenging behaviors exhibited by the child. It is through this collective effort that a comprehensive and accurate FBA is developed.

Parents hold specific rights regarding their child's FBA. They have the right to request an FBA if they believe it is necessary to address their child's challenging behaviors effectively. Also, parents can and should provide valuable input and information regarding their child's behavior, as their insights are essential to understanding the child's behavior comprehensively. Furthermore, parents should be informed and actively involved in the FBA process, including attending meetings and participating in decisions regarding interventions. Finally, parents retain the right to review and provide feedback on the FBA report and the resulting BIP to ensure that their child receives the most appropriate and effective support and accommodations[48].

Functional Skills

Functional skills refer to the practical abilities that individuals need to perform daily tasks and engage in meaningful activities. These skills encompass a wide range of abilities, including communication, social interaction, self-care, problem-solving, and decision-making. Functional skills are essential for promoting independence, autonomy, and participation in various aspects of life.

The importance of functional skills lies in their role in facilitating meaningful participation and inclusion in society. These skills empower individuals to navigate daily routines, interact with others, and achieve a level of independence that enhances their quality of life. For children with autism, developing functional skills is especially crucial as it equips them with the tools they need to thrive in different environments and engage in various activities.

Parents can foster functional skills at home by creating a supportive and structured environment that encourages independence and skill development. They can incorporate everyday activities into their child's routine, such as meal preparation, household chores, and self-care tasks, to promote skill acquisition. Additionally, parents can provide opportunities for social interaction, communication, and problem-solving through play, games, and family activities. By reinforcing and practicing functional skills in the home setting, parents can help their child generalize these skills to other contexts and promote independence.

Teachers can implement functional skills in the school setting by embedding them into the curriculum and daily routines. They can create structured learning activities that target specific functional skills, such as following instructions, organizing materials, and participating in group activities.

Teachers can also incorporate opportunities for social interaction and collaboration into classroom activities to promote communication and social skills development. Individualized Education Programs (IEPs) or 504 plans can be used to identify specific functional goals and accommodations to support students with autism in the classroom. By providing a supportive and inclusive learning environment that focuses on functional skill development, teachers can help students with autism build the necessary skills to succeed academically and socially.

Functions of Behavior

The functions of behavior refer to the underlying reasons or purposes behind why individuals, including children with autism, engage in specific behaviors[6]. These functions are crucial to understand as they can guide parents, teachers, and therapists in developing effective strategies to support individuals. There are four primary functions of behavior:

Escape/Avoidance: Behaviors serving the function of escape or avoidance are used to remove or avoid situations, tasks, or demands that they find challenging, unpleasant, or overwhelming. Examples- A child with autism might engage in tantrums to escape a difficult academic task such or refusing to attend social events to avoid sensory overload.

Attention-Seeking: Behaviors with the function of attention-seeking are used to gain the attention, interaction, or engagement of others. Individuals may display these behaviors when they feel isolated or crave Examples - A child may interrupt conversations to gain attention from caregivers or displaying disruptive behavior to garner the attention of peers during group activities.

Access to Tangibles: Behaviors aimed at gaining access to specific objects, activities, or preferred items fall under this category. Individuals use these behaviors to obtain something they desire.
Examples - A child might engage in repetitive requests to access a favorite toy or exhibiting a tantrum to obtain a snack or a specific food item they like.

Sensory Stimulation: Some behaviors serve the function of sensory stimulation or self-soothing. Individuals engage in these behaviors because they provide sensory input or sensory satisfaction.
Examples - Repeating a specific movement, such as hand-flapping, to self-regulate sensory input or stimming behaviors like rocking or spinning to seek sensory comfort.

Understanding these functions of behavior is necessary for behavior analysts, therapists, and caregivers. It enables them to assess why a particular behavior occurs and tailor interventions accordingly. By addressing the underlying function, they can develop strategies to teach more appropriate behaviors, provide alternatives, or modify the environment to reduce the occurrence of challenging behaviors and promote positive outcomes for individuals, including those with autism.

NOTES

Gastrointestinal Issues

Gastrointestinal (GI) issues are common in the general population but appear to be particularly prevalent among individuals with autism[49]. These issues include constipation, diarrhea, abdominal pain, and bloating, which can cause significant discomfort and distress.

Why are children with autism more likely to experience these GI problems? Research suggests several theories, but the exact reasons aren't entirely clear. One theory involves the gut-brain connection, a two-way communication system between the gut and the brain. In autism, this communication might be disrupted, leading to GI problems. Another theory considers diet and food sensitivities. Children with autism often have limited diets or specific food preferences, which can lead to nutritional imbalances and digestive issues.

Behavioral factors also play a role. Some children with autism may have difficulty communicating their discomfort, leading to undiagnosed and untreated GI issues. GI problems can significantly affect quality of life, making it hard for children to focus in school or enjoy family activities.

Addressing these issues requires a team approach, including pediatricians, gastroenterologists, dietitians, and behavior therapists. Each professional brings a piece to the puzzle, from medical management to dietary changes and behavior interventions. Working together holistically can make a significant difference in the lives of children and their families.

Generalization

Generalization is the ability to apply skills learned in one situation to different scenarios. It is crucial for helping children with autism adapt learned behaviors to new environments, people, or challenges. For instance, a child who learns to greet their therapist with a "Hello!" should be able to use that greeting at school or with family members. Without generalization, each new interaction would require relearning the greeting as if it were a new skill each time[50].

Parents can promote generalization at home by providing diverse and repeated opportunities for their child to practice skills in different settings. For example, if a child learns a communication skill in therapy, parents might encourage the child to use it during family gatherings or while interacting with neighbors. Involving familiar and new people in these practice sessions can also help. Consistency and reinforcement are key to ensuring the child feels comfortable and supported while applying new skills in various situations.

Teachers can foster generalization in school by integrating learned skills across different subjects and social interactions. This might involve coordinating with the child's therapists to understand specific skills and strategies and then applying these in the classroom. Teachers can use role-playing and group activities to simulate real-life scenarios, allowing the child to practice and generalize skills with different peers in various settings. Creating a supportive classroom environment that encourages trial and error and provides positive reinforcement can significantly enhance a child's ability to generalize skills effectively.

Guardianship

Navigating guardianship can be complex but is essential for parents of children with significant disabilities, especially as they approach adulthood. Guardianship means officially becoming the decision-maker for an adult child who cannot make all their life decisions independently.

The journey towards obtaining guardianship begins when the child nears 18. Parents need to gather crucial information, such as medical records, evaluations, and recommendations from healthcare providers or educators. Consulting with a legal expert, preferably a lawyer specializing in guardianship, is imperative. This expert helps parents understand and navigate the legal process, which involves filing a petition for guardianship with the court.

The court process includes interviews, assessments, and a hearing. If the court agrees that guardianship is necessary and in the best interest of the individual, it grants guardianship. Starting the planning when the child is around 17 years old allows for a smoother transition and ensures all necessary arrangements are in place by the time the child reaches adulthood.

Teachers can be allies by sharing critical information about the child's behavior, academic progress, and social interactions. Their input is essential for assessing the child's needs during the guardianship evaluation. They can assist in preparing detailed reports and documentation about the child's development that will be useful in legal settings. Teachers can guide parents to local resources, offer moral support, and advocate for the child's best interests. Informing parents about relevant training sessions and workshops can help demystify the complexities of legal guardianship.

While obtaining guardianship can be complex, it is crucial for ensuring the well-being of a child who may not be able to make all their life decisions independently. With the right preparation, guidance, and resources, parents can navigate this journey effectively.

NOTES

Help

For parents and teachers of children with autism, the journey is often rewarding but can also be challenging and overwhelming. In such cases, asking for help is not just a suggestion—it's a requirement. Understanding the importance of seeking assistance and recognizing when it's needed can make a significant difference in both the child's development and the caregiver's well-being.

Asking for help is crucial because it brings additional resources and perspectives that can enhance a child's learning and development. Specialized knowledge from therapists, insights from other parents, or practical tips from teachers can provide strategies that improve outcomes for children with autism. Furthermore, asking for help can prevent feelings of isolation by connecting with others who understand the challenges faced by those caring for children with autism.

It's important to recognize that asking for help is a sign of strength and resourcefulness, not a weakness. Just as professionals in any field collaborate and consult with peers, so too should parents and teachers managing the complexities of autism. The consequences of not seeking help can be significant. Without support, parents may experience burnout, stress, and frustration, which can inadvertently affect their ability to provide optimal care and education. Over time, this can lead to decreased effectiveness in managing behavioral challenges and supporting the child's development.

There are several indicators that can be a sign that you might need help. Feeling consistently overwhelmed, noticing that your strategies are not effectively addressing the child's needs, or feeling isolated in your experiences are all indicators that it might be time to reach out. Other signs include changes in your own mental health, such as increased anxiety or depression, or feeling ill-equipped to handle new behaviors or educational challenges that arise.

Creating a support network is vital. This network can include therapists, other parents, special education professionals, and online communities. These resources can offer not just emotional support and practical advice, but also camaraderie and mutual encouragement. Together, they enrich the caregiving and educational environments, fostering better outcomes for children and ensuring that those who teach and care for them are also supported.

Hope

Hope fuels persistence, inspires patience, and fosters resilience in the face of challenges. It involves anticipating positive outcomes in the future, even when current circumstances might suggest otherwise. Hope is crucial for maintaining motivation and energy over the long journey of nurturing a child's development.

For parents and educators, maintaining hope is vital because it allows them to envision a fulfilling future for the children they care for, despite the difficulties encountered along the way. Hope is not just wishful thinking; it's a proactive stance that encourages individuals to believe in the potential for growth and learning, which is especially important given the varied developmental trajectories of children with autism.

During tough times, reminders to maintain hope can come from various sources. Success stories of other children with autism, progress milestones, however small, and supportive communities that emphasize possibilities rather than limitations can all reinforce hope. Educators and parents can remind each other to celebrate every step forward, acknowledging that each achievement is a building block for future success.

Having hope also means accepting that the things we wish for might not arrive on our preferred timeline. Hopefulness understands that while progress might be slow, it is nonetheless progress. This type of hope is not passive; it requires active engagement and a commitment to continue trying new strategies and approaches, even when the path forward seems unclear.

For parents, hope might look like celebrating small victories, such as a child learning a new word or mastering a routine task. It's found in the daily commitment to their child's growth and the quiet confidence that their efforts will lead to greater independence and joy in their child's life.

For teachers, hope manifests as a belief in every student's ability to learn and succeed, tailored to each child's needs and timelines. It involves setting realistic, achievable goals for their students and recognizing the importance of each small step toward these goals. Hope in educational settings is also shared collectively—celebrated with colleagues and communicated to students to inspire them and build their self-esteem.

Hyperresponsiveness

Hyperresponsiveness refers to an exaggerated or intensified response to sensory stimuli[51]. This concept is rooted in the sensory processing differences often observed in individuals with autism.

Imagine this: You're sitting in a room where the ticking of a clock sounds like a hammer on an anvil, or a gentle brush of fabric feels like sandpaper scraping your skin. For someone with hyperresponsiveness, everyday sensory inputs—like lights, sounds, textures, or even tastes—can be overwhelming or even cause painful discomfort.

This heightened sensory experience can manifest in various ways. A child with hyperresponsiveness might cover their ears and scream in a noisy environment, refuse to wear certain clothing because of its texture, or be extremely picky with foods due to their taste or texture. These reactions are not behavioral issues but responses to the intense way their nervous system processes these sensory inputs.

For parents whose child exhibits hyperresponsiveness, creating a soothing home environment is key. This involves understanding and minimizing sensory triggers. Using soft, natural fabrics in clothing and bedding can reduce discomfort. Dimming bright lights or using color filters can help manage light sensitivity, and reducing background noise or providing noise-canceling headphones can assist with sound sensitivities. Offering a variety of foods in different textures and tastes, while allowing the child to choose what they are comfortable eating, can also be beneficial. Parents should observe and note what specific stimuli trigger their child's responses and adjust their home environment accordingly to create a more comforting and supportive space[52].

Teachers can support hyperresponsive students by adapting the classroom environment and their teaching methods. This might involve creating a sensory-friendly corner equipped with noise-reducing headphones, soft lighting, or sensory toys that students can use when feeling overwhelmed. Teachers can also implement a flexible dress code that accommodates sensory-friendly clothing and use visual aids and clear, concise instructions to reduce cognitive overload. It's important for teachers to work closely with each child's support team to understand their specific needs and integrate strategies that help minimize sensory overload in the classroom. Regular breaks and a structured routine can also help these students manage their sensory experiences more effectively during the school day.

Hyporesponsiveness

Hyporesponsiveness refers to a reduced or muted response to sensory stimuli[52]. This is equally important in understanding the sensory processing variations often observed in individuals with autism.

Imagine being in a bustling café where everyone is chatting, and the espresso machine is whirring, but to someone who's hyporesponsive, this vibrant environment might barely register. They might not react to sounds that would typically get attention, like their name being called, or they may not feel temperature changes or pain in the way others do.

In everyday life, this might look like a child who doesn't respond to extreme temperatures or doesn't notice when they get a cut or a bruise. They might not react to physical touch in the expected way, seeming indifferent to hugs or physical contact. In a classroom setting, such a child might not turn around when addressed or might continue sitting undisturbed amidst loud noises or activities that would typically cause discomfort or distraction to others.

Hyporesponsiveness can have significant implications for safety, social interactions, and learning environments. For instance, a child who is hyporesponsive might not react to a dangerous situation, like a hot stove, or might not engage with peers in a typical manner, affecting social development.

Recognizing and accommodating hyporesponsiveness involves creating strategies that safely heighten sensory input to match the individual's sensory processing needs. This could include using more pronounced or varied sensory experiences to engage them effectively.

For parents managing a child with hyporesponsiveness, engaging the child's senses in a safe and controlled manner is essential. Parents can introduce sensory-rich activities at home to stimulate their child's sensory processing. Playing with tactile toys like sand, water beads, or play dough can help. Providing opportunities for movement such as bouncing on a trampoline, swinging, or other proprioceptive activities can also be beneficial. Using strong flavors and textures in foods can encourage better eating habits and sensory awareness. It's important for parents to gradually and consistently introduce these sensory experiences, monitoring their child's responses and adjusting the activities to suit their comfort and engagement levels.

Teachers can support students with hyporesponsiveness by incorporating sensory integration techniques into the classroom routine. This might include using weighted vests or lap pads to provide proprioceptive feedback, arranging for structured physical activity breaks that involve stretching or jumping, or using textured materials and fidget toys during lessons to help maintain focus. Teachers should also consider the classroom layout—ensuring there are opportunities for the child to engage physically with the environment in a controlled way, such as through sensory paths on the floor or interactive wall panels. Collaboration with occupational therapists can provide additional strategies tailored to each child's needs, helping to enhance their sensory processing and engagement in school activities. Regularly scheduled, structured sensory activities can help children with hyporesponsiveness become more attuned to their environments and improve their learning experiences.

NOTES

IDEA (Individuals with Disabilities Education Act)

The Individuals with Disabilities Education Act (IDEA) is a federal law in the United States that ensures students with disabilities are provided with Free Appropriate Public Education (FAPE) tailored to their individual needs. Originally enacted in 1975, IDEA has been revised several times to improve its effectiveness and coverage. This law guarantees educational rights to children with disabilities and ensures they receive special education and related services[53].

IDEA is crucial because it provides a legal framework to ensure children with disabilities have access to education similar to that of non-disabled children. It aims to level the educational playing field by providing specific protections and supports. The act recognizes the need for Individualized Education Programs (IEP) and the importance of parent and teacher involvement in crafting education that meets the needs of each child.

IDEA is divided into four main sections:

Part A: General Provisions: This section outlines the general principles and policies, definitions, and overall objectives of IDEA, including the commitment to provide FAPE.

Part B: Assistance for Education of All Children with Disabilities: This section covers educational guidelines for children aged 3 through 21. It outlines the requirements for public schools to serve eligible students with disabilities. Part B also details the processes for evaluation, eligibility determinations, IEP development, and procedural safeguards.

Part C: Infants and Toddlers with Disabilities: Part C addresses the needs of children from birth through age two. This section provides guidelines for early intervention services, which are crucial in supporting the developmental progress of infants and toddlers with disabilities.

Part D: National Activities to Improve Education of Children with Disabilities: This section supports various national activities designed to improve the education of children with disabilities. These activities include professional development, research and dissemination of information, and technical assistance.

Parents should actively engage in understanding and utilizing the rights afforded under IDEA. This involves participating in IEP meetings, understanding evaluation processes, and knowing how to appeal decisions or resolve disputes. Being informed about their child's educational rights and the services the school offers is essential. Effective advocacy includes communicating with educators, staying informed about educational practices and legal rights, and consulting with special education advocates or attorneys when necessary.

For teachers, upholding the principles of IDEA is not only a legal obligation but also a professional and ethical one. Implementing IDEA effectively requires understanding the specific educational accommodations and modifications that each student needs. This can lead to more effective teaching strategies and improved student outcomes. Teachers should collaborate with colleagues, utilize supports and resources provided under IDEA, and engage with parents to create a holistic approach to education that benefits every student.

IEP (Individualized Education Program)

An Individualized Education Program (IEP) is a crucial component of IDEA. It is a detailed and legally binding document developed for each public school child in the U.S. who qualifies for special education. The IEP outlines specific educational goals, the services the school will provide, and how progress will be measured[54].

A student's IEP is designed to ensure they have access to a Free Appropriate Public Education (FAPE) in the least restrictive environment. It provides personalized education plans that address each child's learning styles, challenges, and strengths. The IEP process involves collaboration among parents, teachers, school administrators, and, when appropriate, the students themselves.

The IEP process includes several key steps:

Evaluation: The process begins with a thorough evaluation or assessment of the student to determine their eligibility for special education services under IDEA. This evaluation assesses all areas related to the child's suspected disability.

Eligibility Determination: Based on the evaluation results, a team determines whether the child qualifies for special education services. If the child is found eligible, the IEP development process begins.

IEP Meeting: An IEP meeting is scheduled with the participation of the IEP team, which includes the child's parents, special education teachers, at least one of the child's regular education teachers, a school district representative knowledgeable about the resources available, and others as needed.

IEP Document Development: During the IEP meeting, the team develops the IEP document. This document includes the child's current performance levels, educational goals for the school year, special education supports and services (such as therapies), accommodations, and how the child's progress will be measured.

Implementation
After the IEP is agreed upon, the school is responsible for its implementation. Teachers and school staff must follow the IEP's specifications to support the child's education.

Review and Adjustment
The IEP is a living document and must be reviewed annually48 to update goals and make revisions based on the child's progress and evolving needs. Additionally, the child must be reevaluated every three years to determine continued eligibility48.

Parents play a critical role in the IEP process. They should prepare for IEP meetings by gathering relevant information, observations, and possibly outside evaluations. During meetings, they should feel empowered to ask questions, suggest modifications, and express concerns. Advocating for their child includes ensuring the school follows the IEP as agreed and pushing for reevaluation if they believe their child's needs have changed.

For teachers, adhering to the IEP is essential for meeting the educational needs of students with disabilities. By following the IEP, teachers help ensure that students can access the curriculum at a level appropriate to their needs and abilities. Upholding the IEP not only supports legal compliance but also enhances instructional effectiveness, fosters inclusivity, and promotes educational equity. Teachers should collaborate with the IEP team, participate actively in IEP meetings, and seek continuous professional development to better serve students with IEPs.

Imitation

Imitation is a critical component in the development of children with autism, serving as a versatile tool that enhances various aspects of learning[55]. This process is instrumental in several key developmental areas:

Foundation for Social Learning: Imitation is crucial for developing social skills. As children with autism mimic actions, expressions, and speech, they learn essential social behaviors. This mimicking helps them understand how to engage with others, interpret social cues, and comprehend the nuanced interpretations of body language and facial expressions, which are vital for meaningful interactions.

Language and Communication Skills: Imitation acts as a bridge to communication for children with autism, who often struggle with verbal skills. Starting with simple sounds and progressing to words and sentences, imitation allows these children to gradually build their language capabilities, echoing the world around them until they develop their own voice.

Behavioral Flexibility: For children with autism, engaging in repetitive behaviors is common. Through imitation, they can learn new actions and routines, broadening their behavior repertoire. This expansion is akin to adding new moves to their routine, enhancing their adaptability and flexibility.

Emotional Development: Imitation enables children with autism to recognize and replicate emotions. By copying facial expressions and emotional responses, they learn to decode and empathize with the emotions of others, enhancing their emotional intelligence and understanding.

Motor Skill Development: Beyond social and emotional realms, imitation helps in physical development. Copying movements improves motor skills, coordination, and body awareness, providing a holistic workout that benefits both the brain and body.

Therapeutic Use: In therapeutic settings, such as those involving Applied Behavior Analysis (ABA), imitation is a fundamental technique. It is employed to teach a variety of skills, from simple gestures to complex behaviors, serving as a foundation for more sophisticated learning objectives.

Cognitive Development: Imitation also promotes cognitive development. Children with autism engaging in imitation learn about cause and effect, enhance their problem-solving skills, and refine their decision-making abilities. Each act of imitation adds a piece to the puzzle, helping them form a more comprehensive understanding of their environment.

Parents can leverage imitation to enhance learning by engaging in activities that encourage mimicry, such as cooking, where children can imitate simple tasks like stirring or chopping under supervision. Reading stories with expressive voice changes and physical movements also encourages children to imitate these nuances, aiding language and emotional development. Parents can also incorporate play activities that involve mimicking animal sounds or role-playing scenarios, which are fun yet educational.

Teachers can integrate imitation into their educational practices by demonstrating specific tasks and allowing students to mimic these actions. This could be in academic settings, such as solving math problems step-by-step, or in physical education, where students learn new sports by copying movements. Role-playing in language arts or social studies helps students practice social interactions and develop communication skills. Additionally, teachers can model positive social behaviors for students to imitate, fostering a classroom environment of respect and inclusivity.

Inclusion

Inclusion is an educational philosophy and practice that promotes the active participation of all individuals, regardless of their abilities, in diverse learning and social environments. It is founded on the principle that every person, including those with disabilities, should have the opportunity to engage fully and meaningfully in all aspects of life, including education, employment, and community activities. Inclusion goes beyond physical presence; it aims to create a sense of belonging and acceptance for everyone, respecting their differences and strengths[56].

Inclusion offers many benefits, not only for individuals with disabilities but for society as a whole. It fosters empathy, understanding, and acceptance among peers, promoting a more inclusive and compassionate society. For individuals with disabilities, inclusion provides opportunities for social interaction, skill development, and increased self-esteem. It also allows them to access a broader range of educational and vocational opportunities, ultimately enhancing their quality of life[57].

Inclusion is appropriate in various settings such as schools, workplaces, and community organizations. In educational contexts, it is generally suitable for students of all abilities, as it promotes diversity, peer learning, and social development. Inclusion can also be effective in the workplace, where it encourages a diverse and collaborative workforce, leading to increased innovation and productivity.

While inclusion is a valuable approach, there are instances where it may not be appropriate. In some cases, individuals with severe and complex disabilities may require specialized supports and settings to meet their specific needs. It's essential to strike a balance between inclusion and providing tailored services when necessary to ensure the best outcomes for all individuals.

Creating Opportunities for Inclusion

For parents:

Enroll in Inclusive Extracurricular Activities: Choose programs like art classes, music lessons, or sports where children of all abilities participate together.

Participate in Community Events: Encourage participation in community gatherings, festivals, or charity events that welcome participants of all abilities.

Arrange Playdates: Organize social interactions with children from school or the neighborhood who have diverse abilities.

Visit Inclusive Playgrounds: Spend time in playgrounds that are designed for accessibility, allowing children of all abilities to play together.

Encourage Mixed-Ability Groups for School Projects: Work with teachers to ensure that group assignments include students with varying abilities.

Join Inclusive Scouting or Youth Groups: Look for scouting groups or similar organizations that support and encourage inclusion.

Volunteer Together: Engage in volunteer activities that accommodate children of all abilities, promoting a sense of community and service.

Advocate for Inclusive Policies at School and Clubs: Participate in PTA meetings or board meetings to advocate for inclusive practices in school and extracurricular clubs.

Promote Participation in Religious or Cultural Activities: Ensure that activities organized by your cultural or religious community are accessible and inclusive.

Support Inclusion in Virtual Spaces: Facilitate participation in online communities and activities that are designed to be inclusive.

For Teachers:

Differentiate Instruction: Tailor lessons to accommodate different learning styles and abilities, ensuring that all students can access the curriculum.

Use Cooperative Learning Strategies: Implement group work that encourages collaboration between students of all abilities.

Employ Universal Design Principles: Design classroom materials and activities that can be accessed and understood by students with diverse needs.

Facilitate Peer Supports: Organize peer mentoring or buddy systems that promote social interaction and academic support.

Provide Adaptive Technologies: Utilize technology that can assist students with disabilities in participating fully in classroom activities.

Create an Accepting Classroom Culture: Foster a classroom environment that celebrates diversity and encourages empathy and understanding among students.

Implement Individualized Education Plans (IEPs): Follow IEPs closely and incorporate the recommended accommodations and modifications.

Continuous Professional Development: Engage in ongoing training on inclusive education practices and disability awareness.

Communicate Regularly with Parents: Maintain open lines of communication with parents to ensure consistency in supporting the student's educational and social development.

Encourage Inclusive Extracurricular Activities: Support and promote the participation of students with disabilities in school clubs, sports, and other activities.

By implementing these strategies, teachers not only enhance the educational experience for students with disabilities but also enrich the learning environment for all students, teaching them important lessons in inclusivity and respect for diversity.

Insomnia

Insomnia and sleep difficulties are common in individuals with autism, significantly impacting their daily lives and overall well-being. Research indicates that between 50-80% of children with autism experience some form of sleep disturbance, with insomnia being a particularly common challenge. These sleep issues can range from difficulty falling asleep to frequent awakenings during the night and early morning[58].

Sleep disturbances effect children with autism in numerous ways. Insufficient sleep can worsen behavioral challenges, such as increased irritability, aggression, and hyperactivity. It also affects cognitive functions, impacting attention, memory, and learning abilities. This can hinder their educational and developmental progress. Additionally, the sleep issues of a child with autism can increase stress and fatigue for the entire family, including parents and siblings.

To address these challenges, parents can adopt several strategies. Establishing a consistent bedtime routine is crucial, as it helps signal to the child that it's time to wind down. Activities like reading or listening to soft music can aid in relaxation. The bedroom should be quiet, comfortable, and conducive to rest, with adjustments made to factors like room temperature, lighting, and noise levels to suit the child's sensory preferences. Monitoring diet and daily activities is also important. Limiting caffeine intake and reducing stimulating activities, such as screen time before bed, can be beneficial. Incorporating regular physical activity during the day can promote better sleep at night. Relaxation techniques like mindfulness or gentle yoga can also help prepare the mind for rest.

Insomnia can also significantly impact learning and behavior in the classroom. Teachers can offer support by understanding how sleep deprivation affects a child's irritability, concentration, and memory retention. Creating a calm and structured environment can reduce anxiety, which otherwise often exacerbates insomnia. This tactic includes managing sensory stimuli, controlling noise levels, organizing the physical space to minimize clutter, and using soothing colors and lighting. Incorporating relaxation techniques into the school day, such as guided imagery, deep breathing exercises, or gentle physical activities like stretching, can help alleviate stress and promote better sleep. Encouraging regular physical activity during school hours can also play a role, as it can improve nighttime sleep quality.

Communication with parents is vital; teachers should share observations about the child's sleep-related challenges and discuss strategies that may improve their sleep hygiene. Furthermore, teachers might need to adjust academic expectations when sleep issues are affecting the child's performance. Reducing homework loads or modifying assignments can prevent added stress. For younger children, if aligned with school policies and healthcare recommendations, arranging time for short naps during the school day could also be beneficial.

If sleep issues persist, consulting healthcare professionals who specialize in autism may be necessary. They can provide tailored advice and may suggest specific interventions. Keeping a sleep diary can also be useful in tracking the child's sleep patterns and identifying potential contributing factors to their insomnia.

Intellectual Disability

Intellectual disability is characterized by significantly impaired intellectual and adaptive functioning, with these limitations becoming evident during the developmental period. This definition focuses on three main aspects:

Intellectual Functioning: Often measured by IQ tests, intellectual functioning refers to the ability to learn, reason, make decisions, and solve problems. An intellectual disability typically involves an IQ score below 70 or 75[59].

Adaptive Functioning: This includes the skills necessary for day-to-day living, such as communication, social participation, and independent living. Individuals with intellectual disabilities often experience challenges in these areas.

Developmental Period: Intellectual disabilities are identified during the developmental period, typically before the age of 18.

Autism is a separate condition primarily characterized by challenges in social interaction, communication, and restricted or repetitive behaviors or interests. While intellectual disability and autism can co-occur, they are distinct diagnoses. Some individuals with autism may also have an intellectual disability, but others may not. The severity of autism spectrum disorder varies widely, with some individuals having significant cognitive impairments, while others have average or above-average intelligence.

NOTES

Joint Attention

Joint attention is a fundamental aspect of human communication and social interaction, serving as a cornerstone in the development of social and language skills. It refers to the shared focus of two individuals on an object or event. This shared focus is achieved when one person alerts another to an object via eye gazing, pointing, or other verbal or non-verbal indications. Imagine two people looking at a painting together; one might point to a particular detail, prompting the other to follow their gaze. This simple act creates a connection, a shared understanding about what is being observed[60].

In the context of autism, joint attention is a critical area of focus because individuals with autism often show differences in developing this skill. Typically, joint attention begins to develop in infancy. Babies learn to follow their caregiver's gaze or gestures, which helps them understand that they can share experiences with others. It's a foundational block in not only learning language but also in understanding social cues and developing relationships. However, for children with autism, these skills can develop differently or may be delayed[60].

The implications of this variance in joint attention are significant. Since joint attention is linked to language development and social interaction, difficulties in this area can impact a child's ability to communicate effectively and engage socially. For instance, a child who struggles with joint attention may find it challenging to learn from their environment in the same way other children do, as they might not naturally attend to the social cues or share experiences in the same way. This can lead to challenges in learning new words, engaging in play with peers, or even participating in classroom activities.

Therapies and interventions for autism often focus on improving joint attention skills. Techniques might include teaching a child to follow another's gaze or point, or encouraging them to show objects to others. The aim is to help the child understand and participate in this shared experience, which can open doors to more effective communication and social interaction. It's like building a bridge, allowing the child to connect more easily with the world around them.

Journal

Journaling is a valuable tool. It affords the ability to track milestones, progress, and behavior changes. These records can be crucial for assessing the effectiveness of different strategies and interventions. Journals are particularly useful for preparing for IEP meetings, medical appointments, and therapy sessions.

For parents and teachers, journaling also offers a private space to process their emotions. Writing about daily experiences can help manage stress, celebrate successes, and work through frustrations. This practice can lead to greater self-awareness and a better understanding of their impact on the child's development.

Sharing journal insights between parents and teachers can improve communication and provide a more complete view of the child's experiences. This collaboration can lead to more coordinated efforts to support the child and ensure consistency in approaches used at home and school.

Journals can also serve as keepsakes, capturing memories of the child's journey. For parents, it's a heartfelt way to remember milestones. For teachers, it's a record of professional and emotional experiences that can inform future teaching practices. Journaling supports emotional coping, memory preservation, and provides a rewarding and insightful component to the care and education of children with autism.

Judgement

Managing external judgment is crucial for parents. Often, they face judgment from family, friends, or strangers who may not understand the complexities of autism. Educating others about autism can help to mitigate misunderstandings and foster a more supportive environment. Sharing information and personal experiences can raise awareness and empathy, encouraging a more inclusive and informed community.

However, it's important for parents to recognize their own limits and set boundaries when necessary. Constantly explaining and justifying their child's behaviors and needs can be emotionally and physically taxing. It's perfectly acceptable to step back and protect one's own well-being by choosing not to engage in every conversation or explanation. Parents should prioritize their mental health and avoid burnout by setting clear limits on how much they are willing to educate others.

Teachers may face judgment from colleagues or administrators as well. Advocating for professional development and building alliances with other special education professionals can help. Documenting student progress and strategies used can also provide evidence to support their efforts. Maintaining professional confidence and focusing on the students' needs is essential.

Remember, you are not alone in facing judgment from others. Your dedication, love, and resilience make a profound difference. Lean on supportive communities for solace and practical advice, and never underestimate the power of your own strength and compassion. You are doing an incredible job, and your efforts are making a positive impact. Keep believing in yourself because you got this!

NOTES

Kinetics

Kinetics, the study of motion and movement, holds significant relevance in understanding and supporting individuals with autism. The relationship between kinetics and autism lies in how movement and physical activities can positively impact various aspects of development, including motor skills, sensory processing, social interaction, and emotional regulation[61].

For children with autism, engaging in kinetic activities offers numerous benefits. One benefit is it can help improve motor skills and coordination, which may be challenging for some individuals on the spectrum. Activities such as running, jumping, climbing, and playing sports provide opportunities for children to develop gross motor skills, balance, and spatial awareness.

Kinetic activities can also serve as outlets for sensory integration, helping children with autism regulate their sensory experiences. Many individuals with autism have sensory sensitivities or differences, and engaging in movement-based activities can provide sensory input that is calming or organizing for them. For example, swinging, bouncing on a therapy ball, or engaging in rhythmic movements can help regulate sensory input and promote a sense of calmness and focus.

Furthermore, kinetics can facilitate social interaction and communication skills development. Participating in group activities such as team sports, dance classes, or cooperative games provides opportunities for children to practice turn-taking, sharing, and collaboration with peers. These activities also offer natural contexts for practicing non-verbal communication, such as body language and gestures, which can be particularly beneficial for children with autism who may struggle with verbal communication.

Parents and teachers can incorporate kinetics in various ways to support development and well-being. Here are some strategies:

1. Structured Physical Activities: Incorporate structured physical activities into daily routines, such as taking walks, playing active games, or participating in organized sports. These activities provide opportunities for children to engage in movement while also promoting physical fitness and coordination.

2. Sensory Integration Activities: Create sensory-friendly environments and activities that cater to the sensory needs of children with autism. This might involve providing sensory tools and equipment such as therapy balls, trampolines, or sensory bins filled with tactile materials like sand or rice.

3. Visual Supports: Use visual supports such as visual schedules, timers, or picture prompts to help children with autism understand expectations and transitions during kinetic activities. Visual supports can enhance communication, reduce anxiety, and support independence.

4. Choice and Control: Offer choices and opportunities for autonomy during kinetic activities, allowing children to select activities they enjoy and participate at their own pace. Providing choices empowers children with a sense of control over their experiences and promotes engagement and motivation.

5. Incorporate Interests: Tailor kinetic activities to align with children's interests and preferences. Whether it's playing with a favorite toy, exploring nature, or dancing to preferred music, incorporating children's interests into kinetic activities enhances motivation and enjoyment.

Keyboarding Skills

Keyboarding skills offer invaluable benefits for children with autism, providing an alternative mode of communication and expression that may be more accessible and comfortable than traditional verbal communication. For many children with autism, verbal communication can be challenging due to difficulties with language processing, social communication, or sensory sensitivities. In such cases, learning to navigate a keyboard offers a means of communication that bypasses these barriers, allowing children to express themselves with greater clarity and confidence.

The structured format of written text can provide a sense of predictability and organization that supports communication and comprehension for children with autism. Additionally, the visual and tactile input provided by keyboarding can be particularly beneficial, leveraging their strengths in visual learning and sensory processing. The physical act of typing can also be satisfying and engaging, providing sensory feedback that promotes focus and attention.

To support keyboarding skills development at home, parents can implement several strategies to create an optimal learning environment for their children:

To begin, ensuring access to technology is paramount. Parents should make sure that children have access to devices equipped with keyboards, such as computers, tablets, or specialized communication devices. Additionally, considering purchasing adaptive keyboards or software tailored to individual needs and preferences can further enhance the learning experience.

Second, creating a comfortable workspace is essential. Parents should set up a quiet and comfortable area where children can practice keyboarding without distractions. Providing ergonomic support, such as an adjustable chair and proper keyboard positioning, promotes comfort and ease of use, allowing children to focus on developing their skills effectively.

Incorporating visual supports into the learning process can also be beneficial. Parents can utilize tools such as keyboard overlays, color-coded key stickers, or visual prompts to assist children in locating and identifying letters and symbols on the keyboard. These visual supports enhance learning and facilitate independent navigation of the keyboard, making the learning process more accessible and engaging for children.

Lastly, encourage regular practice to building proficiency over time. Parents should motivate their children to engage in regular practice sessions, starting with simple exercises and gradually increasing complexity as their skills develop. Celebrating progress and accomplishments along the way helps maintain motivation and engagement, fostering a positive learning experience for children as they master keyboarding skills at home.

To effectively support keyboarding skills development in school settings, teachers can implement various strategies tailored to meet the diverse needs of students:

One measure is to integrate keyboarding instruction into the curriculum. Teachers should recognize keyboarding as a valuable skill for communication and academic tasks and incorporate it into literacy activities, writing assignments, and technology lessons. Providing regular opportunities for practice and reinforcement within the curriculum helps students develop proficiency and confidence in keyboarding skills.

Another means of support is by offering access to assistive technology resources. Teachers can provide access to adaptive keyboards, word prediction software, or voice-to-text programs to facilitate the development of keyboarding skills. By tailoring technology tools to meet individual needs and preferences, teachers ensure that all students have access to the support they need to succeed.

An additional step is to offer individualized support and accommodations. If time permits, teachers can provide extra practice sessions, one-on-one instruction, or assistive technology support as needed to ensure students can succeed in learning keyboarding skills. By providing individualized support, teachers empower students to develop the necessary skills and confidence to navigate the keyboard effectively, fostering independence and success in both academic and everyday tasks.

Kudos

Recognize the importance of giving yourself credit and acknowledging your own growth and accomplishments, just as you would for your child or student. As a parent or teacher, you often put immense pressure on yourself to meet high expectations and excel in your role. However, it's important to remember that perfection is not attainable, and everyone makes mistakes along the way. Instead of being too hard on yourself, embrace a growth mindset, recognizing that learning and improvement are ongoing processes. By acknowledging your own growth and progress, you role-model resilience and self-compassion for your children and students.

By giving yourself kudos, you cultivate a positive and supportive environment for yourself and those around you. When you model self-appreciation and self-acknowledgment, you create a culture of positivity and empowerment that encourages children and students to do the same. By fostering an atmosphere of self-celebration, you inspire confidence, resilience, and a sense of accomplishment in your children and students, inspiring them to do the same. Lead by example!

You play a critical role in the lives of your children and students, and you deserve recognition and appreciation for your efforts. By giving yourself kudos and acknowledging your own growth and accomplishments, you demonstrate self-compassion, perseverance, and zeal, which positively impact the well-being and development of your children and students. Just as you celebrate the growth and progress of your child or student, take time to celebrate your own achievements and milestones along the journey of parenthood and education.

NOTES

Language

Children with autism often experience a wide range of language abilities. Some may have delayed speech and struggle with verbal communication, while others might have advanced vocabularies but difficulty with social communication and pragmatic language. This variability underscores the importance of recognizing and addressing each child's needs[62].

To foster language development, it's essential to create an environment that combines sensitivity with directness. For example, using clear and concise language when speaking to a child with autism can help them understand and process information better. However, it's equally vital to be empathetic and patient, recognizing that each child progresses at their own pace.

Engaging in interactive conversations and activities that revolve around the child's interests can be highly effective. Children with autism often have specific topics they are passionate about, and incorporating these interests into learning can make language development more enjoyable. It's like tapping into their own world of enthusiasm.

Incorporating visual supports, such as visual schedules, social stories, and communication boards, can provide structure and aid in communication. These real-world applications of visual aids can help children with autism express their needs and understand social cues better.

Remember that progress may come in small, incremental steps. Celebrate each achievement, no matter how small, and keep the inspirational empowerment alive. Children with autism have immense potential, and with the right guidance and support, they can make significant strides in their language development journey.

Life Skills

First and foremost, teaching life skills to children serves as a cornerstone in their journey towards becoming self-reliant and resilient individuals. These fundamental skills act as the building blocks that form the sturdy foundation upon which their future adulthood is constructed. Just as a solid foundation supports a structure, these life skills provide children with the necessary tools to navigate the complexities of life with confidence and competence. From basic tasks like personal hygiene to more complex responsibilities like managing finances, these skills empower children to take charge of their own well-being and progress towards adulthood. By instilling these skills early on, parents and teachers lay the groundwork for children to face challenges and uncertainties with resilience and determination[63].

These life skills extend beyond mere practicalities; they also foster important qualities such as responsibility, initiative, and adaptability. As children learn to manage their daily routines, make informed decisions, and overcome obstacles, they develop a resilient mindset that equips them to face life's inevitable ups and downs with grace and confidence.

In essence, teaching life skills to children is not just about imparting practical knowledge; it is about empowering them to become capable, confident, and resilient individuals who are prepared to face the challenges of adulthood with courage and determination. It is about laying the foundation for a future where every child has the tools they need to succeed in life. Here are some life skills that can be taught at home and at school[64].

1. Cooking and Meal Preparation: Parents can involve their child in meal planning and preparation, starting with simple recipes and gradually increasing complexity. Teachers can reinforce cooking skills by incorporating cooking activities into classroom lessons or providing resources for cooking at home.

2. Personal Hygiene: Both parents and teachers can reinforce proper hygiene practices by providing visual schedules and reminders. Teachers can also incorporate hygiene lessons into the school curriculum, teaching children about the importance of personal care.

3. Time Management: Parents and teachers can collaborate to establish routines and deadlines using visual schedules and timers. Teachers can incorporate time management activities into classroom lessons, helping children learn to organize their day effectively.

4. Money Management: Parents can introduce basic financial concepts at home, while teachers can reinforce these skills in the classroom through activities like budgeting and saving simulations.

5. Communication Skills: Both parents and teachers can encourage effective communication by providing opportunities for children to practice active listening and expressing themselves clearly. Role-playing scenarios can be used both at home and in the classroom to practice communication skills.

6. Problem Solving and Decision Making: Teachers can provide opportunities for problem-solving exercises and

decision-making activities in the classroom. Collaborative group projects can encourage children to discuss various options and make informed choices.

7. Social Skills: Teachers can incorporate social skills training into the school curriculum, teaching children about greetings, making friends, and resolving conflicts peacefully. Role-playing activities and group discussions can help children practice these skills in a supportive environment. These skills can also be used as children explore extra-curricular activities.

8. Organization Skills: Teachers can help children develop organizational skills by providing tools such as planners and calendars and teaching them how to keep track of assignments and responsibilities. Parents can use similar tools to help children keep track of their chores and personal schedules.

9. Emotional Regulation: Teachers can incorporate lessons on emotional regulation into the classroom, teaching children about relaxation techniques and coping strategies. Providing a calm and supportive classroom environment can also help children manage their emotions effectively. At home children can use these same techniques to navigate emotionally difficult situations.

By working together, parents and teachers can provide the support and guidance needed to develop essential life skills. Through consistent practice, positive reinforcement, and patience, children can build the confidence and independence necessary to navigate the world around them successfully.

Limitations

Understanding and navigating the limitations of a child with autism is a profound aspect of both parenting and teaching. Empathy and patience are fundamental when addressing these limitations. It's essential to acknowledge that children are doing their best, and their limitations do not define their potential. Patience and understanding can significantly aid in helping them overcome obstacles, fostering an environment of acceptance and growth.

Setting realistic expectations is a practical approach for both parents and teachers. While it's important to encourage development and progress, it's equally vital to recognize that some limitations may persist. Maintaining a balance between pushing boundaries and accepting the realities of autism is key, as well as incorporating a touch of humor to remind us that life doesn't always adhere to our plans.

Celebrating even the smallest achievements holds significant importance in supporting children. Inspirational empowerment lies at the core of this approach. Whether it's recognizing a successful attempt at a new skill or improvements in communication, acknowledging and celebrating these moments boosts a child's self-esteem and motivation. It reinforces the notion that progress is achievable, no matter how small or incremental it may seem.

Listen

One of the greatest ways to show respect to a person with autism is to listen to them. Just like any other child, they have thoughts, feelings, and needs that deserve to be heard. Listening also fosters trust and emotional connection. Children may face difficulties in verbal communication, but their non-verbal cues can provide a wealth of information. Real-world application comes into play here as parents and teachers should pay attention to the child's body language, facial expressions, and gestures. For example, if a child is flapping their hands or rocking back and forth, it may be a sign of excitement or sensory overload.

Encouraging non-verbal communication can also be empowering. For instance, using visual supports like communication boards or picture exchange systems can enable non-verbal children to express their desires and needs. This approachability and relatability make the child feel understood and respected.

Additionally, parents and teachers can learn the child's non-verbal cues over time. Each child is different, and their gestures and expressions may have personal meanings. This is where collaboration between parents and teachers becomes helpful. Sharing observations and insights can help create a holistic picture of the child's non-verbal communication.

Literal Thinking

Literal thinking refers to the tendency to interpret language and information in a straightforward and concrete manner, taking words and expressions at face value. For individuals with autism, this cognitive style can be a prominent feature of their communication and thought processes. One of the key aspects of literal thinking is a difficulty in understanding and using figurative language, such as idioms, metaphors, and sarcasm. This can lead to misunderstandings in everyday conversations. For example, when someone says, "It's raining cats and dogs," or "I'm cooler than a polar bear's toenails," a person with literal thinking might envision the animals, rather than understanding the phrases as metaphors[65].

In the context of academics, it's crucial to recognize that literal thinking is not a lack of intelligence or imagination. It is merely a different way of processing information. Individuals with autism often excel in logical and concrete thinking, which can be a strength in certain situations. They may also appreciate clear and direct communication. However, the challenges of literal thinking can sometimes lead to social and communication difficulties. Understanding humor, sarcasm, and implied meanings in conversations can be challenging. Sensitivity and patience are essential when interacting with individuals who have this cognitive style, as misunderstandings can easily occur.

It's important for teachers, parents, and peers to be aware of literal thinking and adapt their communication accordingly. Using clear and concise language, avoiding figurative expressions, and providing explicit explanations, when necessary, can facilitate better understanding.

NOTES

Meltdown

Understanding meltdowns and their causes is critical for parents and teachers to effectively and efficiently support children who are feeling stressed. A meltdown is like a computer system overload—where their brain is bombarded with more input than it can process effectively. Imagine trying to solve an extremely complex puzzle while multiple people are asking questions and loud music blares in the background. This sensory overload is similar to what these children might experience[66].

Meltdowns manifest as intense responses to overwhelming situations and vary from child to child. Common behaviors include crying, yelling, running away, or showing physical aggression. It's important to understand that these are not tantrums or intentional misbehavior but rather the child's way of communicating an inability to cope with the current environment or demands.

At home, a meltdown might occur in a noisy living room with the TV on, during a family gathering, or even during a quiet time if the child feels overwhelmed by daily expectations. In school, meltdowns might be triggered by changes in routine, overwhelming classroom noise, or during transitions between activities. In the community, places like supermarkets, playgrounds, or busy streets can provoke meltdowns due to their sensory-rich environments. When a meltdown occurs, it's essential to approach the situation with patience, empathy, and support, rather than with lectures or punishment. These are moments for calm and understanding, not for correction.

Strategies for Managing Meltdowns

1.   Stay Calm: Your composed presence can help soothe the child. Deep breaths and a calm demeanor can prevent the meltdown from escalating.

2.   Ensure Safety: Make the environment as safe as possible by removing any dangerous objects and making sure the child cannot harm themselves or others.

3.   Reduce Sensory Input: Lowering lights, reducing noise, or moving to a quieter space can help alleviate the overload.

4.   Nonverbal Reassurance: During a meltdown, comforting gestures like a gentle touch or simply being close can provide reassurance without overwhelming the child with words.

5.   Give Space: Sometimes, providing the child with space to process their feelings and calm down is the best approach.

6.   Use Distractions: Offering a favorite toy, blanket, or sensory object can distract from the stressor and provide comfort.

7.   Limit Demands: Keep communication simple and directive without expecting immediate responses during a meltdown.

8.   Identify Triggers: Recognizing and understanding what triggers meltdowns can help in preventing future occurrences or enable you to be more prepared.

9.   Reconnect Post-Meltdown: Once calm is restored, reconnecting through a hug or a favorite quiet activity can reassure the child of their safety and your love.

10. Parent and Teacher Self-Care: Managing meltdowns is challenging. It's vital that caregivers also take time to care for their own emotional and physical well-being.

Both parents and teachers should consider reflecting on past meltdowns to identify possible triggers and signs that precede these episodes. Understanding these can be empowering and can lead to more effective strategies in managing or even preventing future meltdowns. By adopting these approaches, both at home and in school, adults can create a supportive and understanding environment that helps children with autism navigate their world more comfortably.

Modification

The purpose of modifications in an Individualized Education Program (IEP) is a vital topic when it comes to supporting students with special needs. An IEP, including its modifications, is a legally binding document. This means that schools are legally required to provide these accommodations and modifications. It encourages accountability in meeting the educational rights of students with disabilities. At the heart of an IEP is the recognition that every child's educational needs and abilities are unique, especially for children with disabilities. Modifications in an IEP are designed to tailor the educational experience to meet these specific needs. They see to it that the child isn't just included in the educational setting but is actively able to participate and learn effectively[67].

Modifications often involve altering the curriculum and learning expectations to align with the child's abilities and learning style. This could mean changing the complexity of assignments, the way content is delivered, or even the goals and objectives of the curriculum. The idea is to provide a realistic and achievable educational path that acknowledges the child's individual challenges and strengths.

A key purpose of modifications is to ensure that students with special needs have access to the same curriculum as their peers, albeit in a way that is accessible and meaningful for them. It's about leveling the playing field so that these students can engage with the same topics and learning materials, but in a way that accommodates their learning requirements.

Modifications in an IEP also aim to support the overall development of the student, including social, emotional, and behavioral growth. By providing an educational environment that acknowledges and supports their needs, students are more likely to develop confidence, self-esteem, and a positive attitude towards learning. Ultimately, the modifications in an IEP are intended to facilitate the student's long-term educational and personal success. By providing a customized educational approach, these students are better equipped to achieve their full potential, both academically and in their overall personal development.

Teachers play a pivotal role in upholding the effective implementation of modifications. The first step for teachers is to thoroughly review and understand each student's IEP, including being aware of the specific modifications and accommodations outlined, as well as the student's needs, strengths, and goals. Regularly consulting the IEP helps maintain familiarity with its contents. Collaboration with special education teachers, support staff, and related service providers is essential. Regular meetings or check-ins with the special education team can maintain consistency and address any concerns.

When planning lessons, teachers can integrate the modifications into their lesson plans, which might involve altering assignments, providing alternative formats for materials, or adjusting the way information is presented. Creating an inclusive classroom environment also facilitates the implementation of IEP modifications. This might involve arranging the classroom to minimize distractions, providing alternative seating options, or using assistive technology. Be sure to monitor modifications on a regular basis and make adjustments as needed to maintain effectiveness. Teachers can regularly check in with the student to gauge their comfort and success with the accommodations and document any changes or observations to share with the IEP team during review meetings.

Open communication with parents or caregivers is another key element. Regular updates confirm that everyone is on the same page regarding the student's progress and any adjustments that might be needed. Additionally, teachers should advocate for needed resources if they find that additional support is necessary to implement the IEP modifications. This might involve requesting assistive technology, additional staffing, or specific materials that align with the student's accommodations. By following these strategies, teachers can help verify that the modifications listed in their students' IEPs are implemented effectively, providing the necessary support for each student's needs and promoting their academic success.

Motor Skills

Motor skill development in children with autism is a critical aspect that requires attention due to the varied impact autism can have on these skills. It's crucial to understand how both fine and gross motor skills can be affected and to identify ways to support their development[68].

Fine motor skills, which involve the coordination of small muscles in the hands and fingers, can often be challenging for children with autism. For instance, many face difficulties with handwriting, such as holding a pencil correctly or forming letters with precision. Self-care tasks that require fine motor control, like buttoning shirts or tying shoelaces, can also be challenging. Activities like cutting with scissors, coloring, or building with small blocks can both measure fine motor skill development and provide opportunities for improvement. These skills are essential for daily living and independence.

Gross motor skills, on the other hand, involve larger muscle groups and are crucial for activities requiring balance, coordination, and strength. Children with autism may exhibit delays in reaching gross motor milestones such as crawling, walking, or jumping. They might also face challenges in activities that require whole-body coordination, like riding a bike, playing ball games, or running, often appearing clumsy or uncoordinated. Participation in physical activities that are vital for overall health and social interaction can also be impacted.

Addressing these motor skill challenges often involves a combination of therapies and practical activities. Occupational therapy is commonly used to enhance fine motor skills, while physical therapy can significantly aid in developing gross motor skills. These therapies offer targeted exercises aimed at strengthening muscles and improving coordination.

Incorporating motor skill development activities into daily routines at home and school is also beneficial. For fine motor skills, this might include playing with playdough, doing puzzles, or engaging in arts and crafts. For gross motor skills, activities like swimming, playing catch, or navigating obstacle courses can be helpful. In some cases, using adaptive tools or techniques can enable children with autism to perform tasks independently, thereby boosting their confidence and self-reliance.

Music Therapy

Music therapy plays a significant and multifaceted role in supporting children with autism, offering a blend of therapeutic benefits tailored to their specific needs. The primary purpose of music therapy is to use the power of music as a tool to address various developmental areas in children with autism. Music, with its inherent structure and rhythm, provides a predictable and engaging framework that can be immensely comforting for children on the autism spectrum. It creates a non-threatening and enjoyable environment where they can express themselves, learn, and interact[69].

Music therapy is designed to meet individual goals, which may include improving communication skills, enhancing social interaction, reducing anxiety, and promoting emotional expression. For many children with autism, verbal communication can be challenging. Music therapy offers an alternative mode of expression, allowing these children to communicate and express their feelings through music[70].

Here are some benefits of music therapy:

1. Enhancing Communication: Music therapy can significantly aid in developing both verbal and non-verbal communication skills. Singing and vocal play can improve language and articulation skills, while playing instruments can encourage non-verbal expression and communication.

2. Social Skills Development: Group music therapy sessions provide opportunities for social interaction. Participating in shared musical activities can help children with autism learn important social skills such as turn-taking, listening, and engaging with peers.

3. Emotional Regulation: Music can be a powerful tool for emotional expression and regulation. It can help children with autism express their feelings in a safe and controlled environment, and can also be used to teach coping skills for managing emotions.

4. Sensory Integration: Many children with autism have sensory processing challenges. Music therapy can help in modulating sensory responses, offering a structured sensory experience that can be both calming and stimulating as needed.

5. Cognitive Skills: Engaging with music can enhance cognitive abilities such as attention, memory, and problem-solving skills. Music activities that require following sequences or patterns can be particularly beneficial in this regard.

6. Motor Skills Development: Music therapy often involves physical activities like playing instruments, dancing, or other movement to music, which can help in developing both fine and gross motor skills.

Incorporating music into the school day can be incredibly beneficial. One effective strategy for teachers is to use music as a transition tool. Transitions can be challenging for students with autism, but specific songs or melodies can signal changes in activities or settings, easing the process and helping students anticipate what's next. Additionally, integrating music into daily routines can provide structure and predictability. Songs marking key moments of the day, like a "good morning" song to start the day or a "goodbye" song to end the day, can help students understand and participate in routines.

Incorporating movement and dance with music engages students in physical exercise while also providing sensory stimulation. Activities like dancing, clapping, or using musical instruments encourage motor skills development and offer a fun way to experience music. Music can also be a powerful tool for emotional regulation, helping students manage stress or anxiety. Creating a calming playlist or using specific songs to soothe and relax students during times of distress can be effective. Conversely, upbeat music can energize students and help them be alert during tasks that require concentration.

Teachers can also use music to reinforce academic concepts and enhance learning. Songs can be used to teach counting, the alphabet, or other educational topics, making learning more engaging and memorable for students with autism. Group musical activities facilitate social interaction and collaboration, encouraging turn-taking, listening, and cooperation. Adapting musical activities to individual needs is important, as some students may prefer quieter or slower-paced music, while others may enjoy more lively tunes. This flexibility allows students to engage with music in a way that suits them best.

Myth Busters

Let's debunk some common myths about autism and replace them with the facts. It's important to clear up these misconceptions for a better understanding and acceptance of autism.

Myth 1: Autism is Caused by Poor Parenting

Truth: Autism is not caused by poor parenting. It's a neurodevelopmental disorder with genetic and environmental factors. Decades of research have shown that parenting styles do not cause autism[71]. Autism is a complex condition that's present from early childhood and is characterized by differences in brain development.

Myth 2: People with Autism Don't Want Social Interaction

Truth: Many individuals with autism do seek social connections and relationships. The challenge is often in understanding and navigating social norms and cues. They might communicate or interact in different ways, but that doesn't equate to a lack of interest in socializing.

Myth 3: All People with Autism Have Savant Skills

Truth: While some individuals with autism may have exceptional skills or talents (often referred to as savant abilities), this is not the case for everyone with autism. The spectrum is wide, and abilities vary greatly. Most people with autism have a range of skills and challenges like anyone else.

Myth 4: Autism Only Affects Children

Truth: Autism is a lifelong condition. While it is often diagnosed in childhood, its characteristics continue into adolescence and adulthood. Adults with autism may develop coping strategies and thus can present differently than children, but they still have autism.

Myth 5: People with Autism Lack Emotions or Empathy

Truth: Individuals with autism can experience a full range of emotions and can be empathetic. They might express their emotions differently or have challenges in interpreting others' emotions, but this is not indicative of a lack of feeling or empathy.

Myth 6: Autistic People Cannot Lead Independent Lives

Truth: Many individuals with autism can live independent, fulfilling lives. The level of independence can vary greatly depending on the individual's abilities and the support they receive. With appropriate support and accommodations, many people with autism can work, attend college, and live independently.

Myth 7: Autism Symptoms Always Improve with Age

Truth: While some individuals with autism may develop coping strategies and adaptive skills as they age, it's not a given that all symptoms will improve over time. Autism is lifelong, and each person's development is unique. Some challenges may persist, and new ones may emerge.

Myth 8: People with Autism Are Always Intellectually Disabled

Truth: Autism is a spectrum disorder, and intellectual abilities vary widely among individuals. Some may have intellectual disabilities, but others have average or even above-average intelligence. It's important not to generalize about the intellectual capabilities of people with autism.

Myth 9: Autism is Overdiagnosed

Truth: While awareness and understanding of autism have increased, leading to more diagnoses, it doesn't mean the condition is overdiagnosed. Improved diagnostic criteria and greater awareness have allowed more individuals to receive the support and services they need.

Myth 10: Autistic People Are Violent or Dangerous

Truth: There is no evidence to suggest that individuals with autism are inherently violent or dangerous. Like anyone else, some may exhibit challenging behaviors, especially if they are in distress or unable to communicate their needs effectively. These behaviors are not indicative of a general tendency for violence.

Myth 11: A Gluten-Free, Casein-Free Diet Can Treat Autism

Truth: While specific dietary changes (like a gluten-free, casein-free diet) can help some individuals with autism, especially if they have allergies or intolerances, there's no conclusive evidence that such diets can treat autism in general. Dietary changes should be considered on a case-by-case basis and under medical supervision.

Myth 12: Autistic People Have No Sense of Humor

Truth: Many people with autism have a great sense of humor and can enjoy jokes, comedy, and playful interactions. Their sense of humor may be different, or they might have difficulty understanding certain types of humor, but this doesn't mean they lack a sense of humor altogether.

Myth 13: People with Autism Can't Form Close Relationships

Truth: People with autism can and do form deep, meaningful relationships. While they may interact and communicate in ways that are different from neurotypical individuals, this doesn't prevent them from developing close bonds with family, friends, or romantic partners. The key is understanding and respecting their communication and interaction styles.

Myth 14: Autistic Individuals Always Prefer Routine and Hate Change

Truth: While many people with autism find comfort in routine and predictability, it's not a universal trait. Some may be more adaptable or even enjoy novel experiences. It's important not to generalize this preference for routine as being applicable to all individuals with autism.

Myth 15: Autism Affects Only Boys

Truth: While autism is more commonly diagnosed in boys, it certainly affects girls as well. There is growing awareness that autism can present differently in girls, which might lead to under diagnosis or misdiagnosis.

Dispelling these myths is important for a deeper understanding of autism. It fosters appreciation for the challenges and strengths of individuals on the spectrum and promotes a more empathetic and supportive environment for them. It helps in recognizing the diversity and individuality of people on the autism spectrum and challenges stereotypes and misconceptions.

NOTES

Neurodiversity/Neurodivergent

Neurodiversity celebrates variations in human brain functioning. Instead of viewing neurological conditions such as autism, ADHD, dyslexia, and other cognitive differences as "disorders" that need to be corrected or cured, neurodiversity frames them as natural variations in the human experience. This paradigm shift in understanding emphasizes the importance of embracing these differences, much like we celebrate diversity in cultures, personalities, and perspectives[72].

The neurodiversity perspective suggests that the differences in the way individuals think, learn, and process information are simply alternative ways of experiencing the world. It's akin to saying, "Our brains are wired differently, and that's okay!" This approach challenges the medical model, which often focuses on deficits or what people with neurological differences can't do, by instead highlighting their strengths and capabilities. For example, many individuals on the autism spectrum have remarkable attention to detail, deep focus on interests, or exceptional memory – qualities that might be undervalued if only seen through the lens of deficit[73].

Viewing neurological differences as natural variations rather than defects has a profound impact on the identity and self-perception of individuals who are neurodiverse. It shifts the narrative from being "broken" or "abnormal" to being part of a rich tapestry of human diversity. This can enhance self-esteem, reduce stigma, and promote acceptance within both the neurodiverse community and the broader society. Embracing neurodiversity promotes inclusiveness. It advocates for environments that cater to different needs and learning styles, whether in schools, workplaces, or communities. By creating settings that accommodate various ways of thinking and being, we not only support neurodiverse individuals but also enrich our shared spaces with diverse talents and perspectives.

The words we choose are important! It plays a crucial role in shaping our understanding and attitudes. The neurodiversity paradigm encourages us to reframe our language, moving away from terms that marginalize, and instead, use language that respects and acknowledges differences. This reframing fosters empathy and understanding which are key components of an inclusive society. By viewing neurological differences as part of the natural variation in the human population, neurodiversity broadens our view of human potential. It encourages us to look beyond traditional measures of success or intelligence and appreciate a wider range of skills, talents, and ways of thinking. This perspective aligns with a more holistic view of human potential, recognizing that everyone has their own contributions to make.

Non-Verbal vs. Non-Vocal

The distinction between "non-verbal" and "non-vocal" is subtle yet significant, especially when we're discussing communication styles, particularly in the context of the autism spectrum and other developmental conditions[74].

"Non-verbal" in the broadest sense refers to communication that occurs without the use of spoken words. This can encompass a wide range of behaviors and actions. For individuals described as non-verbal, this typically means they do not use spoken language as their primary means of communication. However, they may communicate in other ways, such as through gestures, facial expressions, sign language, written communication, or the use of communication aids like picture cards or electronic devices. It's important to note that being non-verbal doesn't mean an inability to make sounds or vocalize; rather, it's about the absence or limited use of conventional speech for communication.

"Non-vocal" is more specific and refers to individuals who do not use their voice to speak. This term is often used to describe those who are physically unable to produce vocal sounds or speech. A non-vocal person might still communicate using other forms of verbal communication, like typing or sign language, and they can be very effective in expressing themselves through these means. The term "non-vocal" is generally focused on the physical ability to produce sound, rather than the broader communicative functions[75].

In the autism community, understanding these distinctions is crucial for providing appropriate support and resources. While non-verbal individuals may benefit from various communication aids and strategies that bypass the need for spoken language, non-vocal individuals might require specific tools or techniques that compensate for their inability to use their voice, yet still utilize verbal communication in a different format. In both cases, the emphasis is on recognizing and valuing diverse forms of communication, allows each individual's way of expressing themselves to be understood and respected.

Nurture

By concentrating on what children excel at and enjoy, we can enhance their sense of self-worth, increase their engagement, and optimize their overall development. This approach not only builds a strong foundation for lifelong learning and adaptation but also deeply enriches their emotional and social well-being.

Focusing on a child's strengths helps build their confidence and abilities, allowing them to navigate the world with increased competence and assurance. For parents, this might mean creating home environments that are tailored to the child's specific interests and sensitivities, ensuring they have the space and support to explore their passions. In the classroom, teachers have the opportunity to integrate these interests into the curriculum, thereby enhancing engagement and providing a bridge between the child's individual world and the broader educational environment. Let's look at some more examples.

At Home

Encourage Special Interests: Children with autism often have intense interests or areas of expertise. Parents can nurture these passions by providing resources, creating projects, or engaging in activities related to these interests. For example, if a child loves trains, parents can take them on train rides, visit train museums, or build model trains together.

Create a Structured Environment: Many children with autism thrive in structured environments. Parents can help by creating predictable routines, setting clear expectations, and using visual schedules or cues. A consistent daily routine provides a sense of security, allowing the child to focus on developing their strengths.

Foster Communication: Communication is important to support a child's preferred mode of communication, whether it's spoken language, sign language, or using communication devices. Encouraging expressive communication can help children with autism share their interests and connect with others.

Promote Sensory-Friendly Activities: Many children with autism have sensory needs. Parents can nurture their strengths by providing sensory-friendly activities and environments, like sensory bins, calming spaces, or outdoor play. Sensory activities can help children regulate their emotions and focus on their strengths.

Celebrate Achievements: Recognizing and celebrating a child's achievements, no matter how small, helps build their confidence and encourages them to pursue their interests and strengths. Positive reinforcement is a powerful tool for nurturing a child's talents and self-esteem.

In the Classroom

Incorporate Special Interests into Learning: Teachers can use a child's special interests as a tool for engaging them in learning. For example, if a student loves dinosaurs, a teacher could incorporate dinosaurs into math problems or writing assignments. This approach not only nurtures the child's passion but also enhances their motivation to learn.

Differentiate Instruction: Differentiated instruction allows teachers to tailor their teaching strategies to meet the diverse needs of students. This might involve using visual aids, hands-on activities, or technology to align with a child's strengths and learning style. Personalized learning helps children with autism succeed academically while also nurturing their abilities.

Provide a Supportive Environment: Creating a supportive classroom environment includes establishing clear routines, providing sensory breaks, and using positive behavior supports. A nurturing environment helps children with autism feel safe and valued, which is crucial for developing their strengths.

Encourage Peer Relationships: Facilitating positive peer interactions can help children with autism develop social skills and build friendships. Teachers can use buddy systems, cooperative learning, or structured social activities to encourage these relationships. Peer support helps children with autism develop interpersonal skills while also providing opportunities to showcase their strengths in a social context.

Focus on Strength-Based Goals: Setting educational goals that focus on a child's strengths, rather than solely on their challenges, can be highly motivating and empowering. Teachers can work with students to set and achieve goals that align with their interests and talents, which fosters a positive and nurturing learning experience.

Both settings require a thoughtful approach that celebrates achievements, big and small, reinforcing the child's progress and encouraging them to stretch their capabilities. By affirming their strengths, we not only acknowledge their potential but also empower them to see themselves as capable and resilient individuals. This nurturing approach is essential for fostering an atmosphere where children with autism can thrive academically, socially, and personally, making the most of their talents and perspectives.

NOTES

Occupational Therapy

Occupational therapy (OT) is a field dedicated to empowering individuals to overcome challenges in their daily lives, particularly those related to their occupations or daily activities. The term "occupation" in this context doesn't just mean a job or profession; it encompasses all sorts of meaningful and necessary activities that occupy one's time, including self-care and leisure activities[76].

For children with autism, occupational therapy is like a bridge that helps them cross over the often-tricky waters of their challenges. Autism presents a specific set of challenges for each child. Here's where OT comes in!

1. Sensory Integration: Many children with autism experience sensory processing issues; they might be overly sensitive to light, sound, or touch, or conversely, might seek out intense sensory experiences. OT can help these kiddos make sense of their sensory experiences, like helping them find ways to deal with loud noises or textures they find icky.

2. Motor Skills Development: Some kids with autism might struggle with fine motor skills (like buttoning a shirt or using a pencil) or gross motor skills (like jumping or running). Occupational therapists devise fun and engaging activities (think play-dough or obstacle courses) to strengthen these skills.

3. Social Skills: Interacting with others can be tricky for children with autism. OTs often use role-playing or group activities to help these kids navigate social situations, understand body language, and learn to share and take turns.

4. Independence in Daily Activities: OT is all about helping children become more independent. This can include self-care skills like dressing, eating, and grooming, or other daily tasks like organizing their schoolwork.

5. Coping Strategies: Occupational therapy also teaches coping strategies for dealing with frustration or anxiety, which can be common in children with autism. This could involve techniques like deep breathing, using a stress ball, or finding a quiet space when things get overwhelming.

6. Play and Leisure Skills: Yes, learning how to play is part of OT! Play is crucial for a child's development and learning. OTs help children with autism learn how to engage in play, use toys appropriately, and even how to have fun (because fun is important!).

In schools, occupational therapy (OT) can be provided as a related service under the Individuals with Disabilities Education Act (IDEA) to support students who have educational needs related to their ability to participate in the school environment. Here's a breakdown of how a student qualifies for OT as a related service:

1. Evaluation and Assessment: The process typically begins with a comprehensive evaluation conducted by a team of professionals, which may include educators, psychologists, speech-language pathologists, and occupational therapists. During this evaluation, the child's abilities and challenges in various areas, including motor skills, sensory processing, self-care, and activities of daily living, are assessed.

2. Identification of Educational Needs: Based on the evaluation results, if it's determined that the student has significant difficulties that impact their ability to access and

benefit from their education, they may be identified as eligible for special education services under IDEA. This eligibility is typically determined through the development of an Individualized Education Program (IEP) or a 504 plan.

3. Identification of OT Needs: Within the IEP or 504 plan, the team identifies the specific areas in which the student requires support. If occupational therapy is deemed necessary to address the student's needs and facilitate their educational progress, it may be recommended as a related service.

4. Documentation of Need: The IEP or 504 plan outlines the goals and objectives for the student, as well as the related services and accommodations necessary to support their educational needs. If occupational therapy is included, the plan will specify the frequency, duration, and type of OT services required.

5. Review and Monitoring: The IEP or 504 plan is reviewed and updated regularly, typically at least annually, to assess the student's progress and determine whether the services and accommodations remain appropriate and effective. Adjustments may be made based on the student's evolving needs and progress.

It's important to note that the criteria for qualifying for OT services as a related service may vary depending on the school district and state regulations. Additionally, eligibility for OT services is based on the student's individual needs and educational goals, rather than a specific diagnosis. Therefore, students with a wide range of conditions and challenges, including but not limited to autism, ADHD, developmental delays, and physical disabilities, may qualify for OT services in school if it's determined to be necessary to support their educational success.

Optimism

The importance of optimism in your life cannot be overstated. It's a powerful force that shapes the entire journey you're on, casting hope and positivity on the path you're navigating alongside these remarkable children. At its core, optimism is like a bright guiding star, illuminating the way forward amidst challenges and triumphs alike.

Optimism isn't just a feel-good attitude; it's a vital ingredient for resilience. Parenting or teaching a child with autism presents its share of ups and downs, and an optimistic outlook acts as a resilient shield. It helps you maintain balance and perseverance, even when faced with daunting challenges. This resilience is not only essential for your own well-being but also serves as a strong foundation from which you can effectively support and advocate for these incredible children.

Optimism is a potent tool in advocacy. When you're optimistic, you become a driven advocate, seeking out resources, support, and opportunities for these children with unwavering determination. Your proactive approach can lead to better outcomes, as you're more likely to explore avenues that encourage their development and inclusion in various aspects of life. The impact of your optimism extends beyond your immediate interactions with children. They are keen observers, and they mirror your attitudes and behaviors. By adopting an optimistic perspective, you inadvertently teach them to approach life's challenges with positivity and resilience. This valuable life lesson goes far beyond managing autism-related challenges; it equips them with essential skills for navigating the broader aspects of life.

In essence, your optimism is a beacon of hope that paves the way for a more fulfilling and enriched life experience for both you and these incredible children. Together, let's continue to nurture a positive and supportive environment where optimism flourishes, and every child can reach their full potential.

Oral Motor

Oral motor issues refer to difficulties in coordinating and strengthening the muscles used for speech, chewing, swallowing, and other oral activities. These challenges are quite common among children with autism and can significantly affect various aspects of their routines. Speech and communication are primary areas affected by oral motor issues. Children with autism may struggle to articulate sounds and form words correctly due to poor muscle control in the mouth and tongue. This can lead to speech delays and difficulties expressing themselves, which can be frustrating for both the child and their caregivers. Speech therapy plays a crucial role in addressing these challenges, focusing on improving oral motor skills and enhancing communication abilities[77].

Chewing and swallowing difficulties are also prevalent among children with autism who have oral motor issues. These challenges may manifest as trouble with certain food textures, gagging, choking, or even refusal to eat certain foods. Occupational therapists and speech-language pathologists collaborate to address these issues by introducing appropriate food textures and teaching strategies to improve chewing and swallowing safety. Sensory sensitivities often accompany oral motor issues as well. They may have heightened sensitivities to tastes, textures, or temperatures of foods, making mealtime overwhelming. Occupational therapists can help children gradually desensitize their sensory responses and expand their food preferences.

In addition to therapy, there are various strategies parents and teachers can implement to support children with autism and oral motor issues. These may include offering a variety of textured foods, using specialized utensils or oral tools to improve muscle strength and coordination, and creating a calm and structured mealtime environment. It's essential to recognize that oral motor challenges can vary greatly among children. Therefore, a personalized approach, often developed in collaboration with speech and occupational therapists, is crucial. Patience, consistency, and understanding are key when working with children who have oral motor issues, as progress may be gradual but incredibly rewarding in enhancing their overall quality of life and communication abilities.

Overstimulation

Overstimulation occurs when a child's nervous system becomes overloaded with sensory information, leading to various behavioral cues. Identifying overstimulation often involves observing these behavioral cues. A child may become increasingly agitated, anxious, or irritable. They might cover their ears, close their eyes, or try to escape the environment. Some children may exhibit repetitive behaviors, like hand-flapping or rocking, as a way to self-soothe when they're overwhelmed. Changes in breathing patterns, such as hyperventilation, can also signal heightened stress[78].

It's important to have a deep understanding of each child's sensory sensitivities and triggers. This awareness allows us to identify situations or environments that might lead to overstimulation. Open communication with the child, if possible, can help them express their discomfort, enabling us to respond promptly. When a child with autism is overstimulated, it's crucial for us to take immediate action to provide comfort and relief. First, we can guide the child to a quieter and less stimulating environment. Reducing sensory input, such as dimming lights, lowering noise levels, or offering a calm, safe space, can be immensely helpful. It's essential to respect the child's need for personal space and allow them to retreat if they wish. We can also employ sensory self-regulation strategies. Gentle pressure, like a hug or a weighted blanket, can provide comfort by grounding the child's sensory experiences. Deep breathing exercises can be practiced together to help the child regain control over their emotions and reduce anxiety.

Additionally, creating a "sensory toolkit" with items that the child finds soothing, such as fidget toys, noise-canceling headphones, or calming sensory objects, can be beneficial. These tools can serve as immediate interventions when overstimulation occurs. Ultimately, the resolution lies in proactive strategies that prioritize understanding the child's sensory needs and responding with empathy and support. By recognizing the signs of overstimulation and providing a nurturing and calming environment, we can help children with autism navigate the challenges of sensory overload effectively, fostering a sense of safety and emotional well-being.

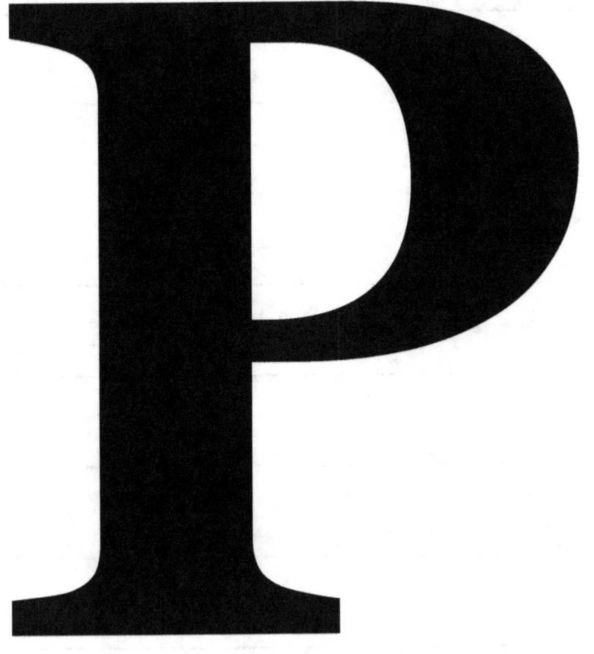

NOTES

PECS (Picture Exchange Communication System)

PECS, which stands for Picture Exchange Communication System, is a well-established and widely used augmentative and alternative communication (AAC) system designed to assist individuals with communication difficulties. It's like giving individuals a visual language to express their needs, wants, and thoughts. Parents of children with autism can use PECS as a powerful tool to facilitate communication, and it can be beneficial for both verbal and non-verbal children. For non-verbal children, PECS provides a way to communicate their needs and desires effectively when spoken language is challenging. For verbal children with limited communication skills, PECS can serve as a bridge to expand their language and expressive abilities[79].

PECS involves using a series of pictures or symbols that represent objects, actions, or concepts. Here's how parents can use PECS effectively at home:

1. Start Simple: Begin with a few basic and highly motivating items or activities that your child is interested in, such as a favorite toy, snack, or activity.

2. Create a PECS Binder or Board: You can create a physical binder or board with Velcro strips where you attach the picture symbols. Place the symbols for the desired items or activities in the binder or on the board.

3. Teach the Exchange: Encourage your child to take a picture symbol (e.g., a picture of a cookie) and hand it to you in exchange for the item or activity they want (e.g., the

actual cookie). This exchange is a fundamental concept of PECS.

4. Use Visual Prompts: Initially, you may need to provide visual prompts or guidance to help your child understand the process. For example, you can point to the picture symbol as you say the word.

5. Reinforce Communication: Always honor your child's communication attempts using PECS. If they hand you a picture symbol, promptly give them what they requested. This positive reinforcement encourages further communication.

6. Expand Vocabulary: As your child becomes more comfortable with PECS, gradually introduce new symbols to expand their vocabulary and ability to express themselves.

7. Consistency is Key: Be consistent in using PECS throughout the day. Encourage your child to use it for various needs and wants, and also for social interactions and sharing experiences.

8. Seek Professional Guidance: If possible, work with a speech-language therapist or AAC specialist who can provide guidance and tailor the use of PECS to your child's specific needs.

Creating PECS at home is a manageable task that can significantly benefit children with autism in their communication development. Parents can take the initiative by starting with simple picture symbols that represent their child's interests or daily activities. They can either make their own symbols using readily available materials or access pre-made PECS symbol libraries online.

Taking photos of actual items and printing them as symbols is another option. Once the symbols are prepared, parents can attach Velcro to the back and place them in a binder or on a board for easy access and organization.

In the school setting, teachers can also play a pivotal role in implementing PECS to support communication and interaction among students with autism. Teachers can collaborate with speech therapists and special education professionals to introduce PECS into the classroom environment. They can create visual schedules, communication boards, and choice boards using PECS symbols to facilitate communication and enhance participation in classroom activities. By incorporating PECS into daily routines and lessons, teachers can provide additional support for students with autism to express their needs, preferences, and ideas effectively.

Both at home and in school, consistency and gradual expansion of PECS use are key. Parents and teachers can work together to reinforce the use of PECS across different environments and activities, helping children with autism generalize their communication skills. Through consistent practice and encouragement, children can develop confidence and independence in using PECS to communicate their thoughts and interact with others, fostering meaningful connections and enhancing their overall communication abilities.

Pediatrician

A pediatrician plays a pivotal role in the care and support families. They often serve as the primary healthcare provider and the first point of contact for parents when it comes to their child's developmental concerns. One of their crucial roles is early identification and diagnosis. Pediatricians are often the first to notice developmental concerns in children. They play a pivotal role in the early identification of autism by conducting developmental screenings and referring children for further assessment when necessary. They may use standardized screening tools like the M-CHAT (Modified Checklist for Autism in Toddlers) to assess risk factors.

Once autism is suspected or diagnosed, pediatricians typically refer the child to specialists such as developmental pediatricians, child psychologists, or pediatric neurologists for a comprehensive evaluation and formal diagnosis. These specialists can provide a more detailed assessment and confirm the diagnosis. Following a diagnosis, pediatricians collaborate with other healthcare professionals and therapists to develop and oversee the child's treatment plan. They may refer families to early intervention services, speech therapy, occupational therapy, or applied behavior analysis (ABA) therapy based on the child's needs.

Pediatricians also play a crucial role in medication management. In some cases, they may prescribe medication to manage specific symptoms or co-occurring conditions related to autism, such as anxiety or attention-deficit/hyperactivity disorder (ADHD). They monitor the child's response to medication and make adjustments as needed. Additionally, pediatricians continue to provide routine medical care, monitor the child's growth and development, and address any health concerns that may arise in children with autism. They also ensure that vaccinations and preventive care are up to date.

Beyond medical care, pediatricians provide valuable parent education and support. They educate parents about autism, its characteristics, and available resources. They offer guidance on managing behavioral challenges, accessing support services, and connecting with local autism organizations. Pediatricians also serve as advocates for the child's educational and healthcare needs within the healthcare system and school settings. They can provide documentation and recommendations to support the child's eligibility for special education services and accommodations.

In the aftermath of their child's autism diagnosis, parents may find it valuable to engage in open and informative discussions with their pediatrician. These conversations can address various aspects of their child's care and support, including treatment plans, referrals, developmental milestones, co-occurring conditions, available resources, educational advocacy, and follow-up appointments. Clear communication with the pediatrician enables the child to receive comprehensive care.

Physical Therapy

Physical therapy is a journey to enhance and restore functional ability and quality of life to those with physical impairments or disabilities. It's a healthcare specialty involving evaluation, diagnosis, and treatment of physical disorders, typically through exercises, hands-on therapy, and various therapeutic modalities. It's about helping people move better and feel better. The need for physical therapy could be the result of an injury, surgery, chronic pain, or a developmental condition. The telltale signs? Difficulty with basic movements like walking, climbing stairs, or carrying objects; chronic pain; joint stiffness; muscle weakness; or a decrease in functional movement[82].

Children with autism often experience challenges that are not just cognitive or social, but also physical. These might include motor skill delays, poor muscle tone, difficulty with coordination, and challenges with sensory processing. For these children, physical therapy is like a tailored exercise program that helps them develop better coordination, balance, strength, and motor skills. It's not just about the physical benefits; these improvements can also boost confidence, self-esteem, and participation in social activities.

Physical therapy for children with autism often involves fun and engaging activities designed to meet their specific needs and preferences. It's a blend of structured exercises and playful, exploratory activities that encourage movement and interaction. The therapist might use sensory integration techniques to help the child process and respond to sensory information more effectively. This can be particularly beneficial for children with autism who may have heightened or reduced responses to sensory stimuli.

Placement

In the realm of education, "placement" refers to the specific educational setting or program where a student is enrolled to receive instruction and support. It's like finding the right puzzle piece that fits a student's educational needs and goals. Placements can vary widely, from general education classrooms to specialized programs for students with disabilities[80]. Here's a breakdown of key aspects related to educational placements:

1. Determining Placements: Placements are determined through a collaborative process involving parents, educators, and school administrators. It begins with an evaluation of the student's educational needs, including academic abilities, learning style, and any special considerations such as disabilities or language proficiency.

Based on this assessment, the Individualized Education Program (IEP) team or 504 Plan team (for students with disabilities) will make placement recommendations. The team considers factors like the least restrictive environment (LRE) that provides appropriate support, the availability of specialized services, and the student's social and emotional well-being.

2. Changing Placements: If a parent believes that their child's current placement is not appropriate or effective, they have the right to request a review of the placement. This can be initiated through the IEP or 504 Plan process. The parent can express their concerns and request a change in placement based on the student's needs. The school team, along with the parent, will reevaluate and discuss potential alternatives to find a more suitable placement.

3. Assessing Appropriateness: To determine if a placement is appropriate for their child, parents can consider several factors:
- Academic Progress: Is the student making reasonable academic progress in their current placement?
- Social and Emotional Well-being: Is the student comfortable, happy, and able to engage socially and emotionally in the current environment?
- Specialized Services: Are the necessary services and support (e.g., speech therapy, special education) available and effective?
- Individual Goals: Is the placement aligned with the student's individual educational goals and needs, as outlined in their IEP or 504 Plan?

It's important for parents to maintain open communication with the school and actively participate in the placement decisions. They should also be aware of their rights under special education laws, such as the Individuals with Disabilities Education Act (IDEA) in the United States, which ensures that students with disabilities receive a free and appropriate public education (FAPE) in the least restrictive environment. It is also beneficial to request an information about all the placement options the school district provides. Don't be afraid to ask why school staff may suggest a certain placement for your child as well as an explanation of why your child doesn't qualify for other placements.

Educational placement is a critical aspect of a student's educational journey, and it should be tailored to meet their needs and promote their academic and social growth. Parents play a vital role in this process by advocating for their child and collaborating with educators to ensure that the chosen placement is the right fit.

Pragmatics

Pragmatics, in the realm of language and communication, is like the unwritten rule book of social interaction. It encompasses the use of language in social contexts, focusing on the ways in which people produce and comprehend meanings through language. This includes understanding and using non-literal language like idioms, humor, and metaphors, as well as knowing what to say, how to say it, when to say it, and to whom it should be said[81].

For many individuals with autism, navigating the intricate world of pragmatics can be like trying to read a map in a foreign language. Autism often involves challenges with social communication, which directly ties into pragmatic language skills. Here are some of the ways pragmatics can be affected in individuals with autism:

1. Difficulty Understanding Non-Literal Language: Idioms, sarcasm, and jokes rely on understanding unspoken cues and shared knowledge. For someone with autism, these can be confusing. It's like everyone else is laughing at a joke they just can't see.

2. Challenges with Social Cues: The ebb and flow of conversation – knowing when to speak, when to listen, how to interpret body language and facial expressions – can be daunting. It's like being in a dance where everyone knows the steps except you.

3. Topic Maintenance and Shifts: Sticking to a topic or smoothly transitioning to another topic in conversation requires a nuanced understanding of social interaction. Individuals with autism might struggle to pick up on cues that it's time to change the topic or may have difficulty moving away from preferred subjects.

4. Understanding Context: The context of a conversation – like where it's happening, who is involved, and the relationship between speakers – shapes its content and tone. For those with autism, deciphering this context isn't always straightforward.

5. Use of Language: Some individuals with autism might use language in a way that seems unusual or idiosyncratic. Their speech might be overly formal, pedantic, or lack the typical back-and-forth of conversations.

The impact of these challenges can be profound. Social interactions, which are often spontaneous and nuanced, can become sources of anxiety and misunderstanding. But here's the empowering part: with support and targeted interventions, many individuals with autism can develop stronger pragmatic skills. Speech and language therapy, social skills training, and real-world practice can all help in learning the subtle art of pragmatics.

Understanding pragmatics in autism is key to supporting effective communication and social interaction. It's about helping individuals with autism decode the rule book of social language, turning what might seem like a maze into a navigable path.

Processing Speed

Processing speed refers to the pace at which an individual can take in, interpret, and respond to information from their environment. It's a fundamental cognitive skill that plays a crucial role in various aspects of daily life, including learning, communication, and social interaction. For children with autism, processing speed can vary significantly, and it's important not to rush them in their responses[83].

One of the key characteristics of autism is the presence of sensory sensitivities and differences in processing information. These differences can affect how quickly a child with autism can process and respond to stimuli, whether it's verbal instructions, social cues, or sensory input. It's important to recognize that the variability in processing speed among children with autism is part of their neurodiversity.

Rushing children with autism to respond can lead to several negative outcomes. It can increase anxiety and stress levels. Imagine being in a situation where you're bombarded with information, and you're expected to respond rapidly. This can be overwhelming for anyone, but it's especially challenging for children with autism, who may struggle with sensory overload and social anxiety. Also rushing children with autism can hinder their ability to fully understand and process information. They may miss important details or fail to grasp the meaning of a conversation or task. This can, in turn, affect their learning, communication, and overall cognitive development.

Instead of rushing, adopt a patient and supportive approach. This approach aligns with the principles of understanding and accommodating their processing styles and sensory sensitivities. It allows the child to engage at their own pace, fostering a more inclusive and less stressful environment. By giving children the time they need to process and respond, we not only reduce their anxiety but also create opportunities for them to participate more actively in various activities. It's important to be patient, use clear and simple language, provide visual supports when necessary, and allow for pauses and breaks during interactions.

Psychiatrist vs. Psychologist

Psychiatrists and psychologists both contribute significantly to the care of children with autism, but their roles and areas of expertise differ considerably. Psychiatrists are medical doctors with specialized training in psychiatry, enabling them to diagnose and treat mental health conditions, including co-occurring issues in children with autism like anxiety and depression. They can prescribe medication when necessary and approach mental health from a medical and neurological perspective. Psychiatrists are also equipped to handle psychiatric emergencies.

On the other hand, psychologists possess expertise in psychology and behavior. They conduct psychological assessments to evaluate a child's cognitive, emotional, and behavioral functioning and can diagnose autism.

Psychologists primarily focus on providing various forms of therapy and intervention, including behavioral therapy and cognitive-behavioral therapy. They specialize in developing behavioral strategies and often collaborate with schools to create tailored educational plans. Psychologists also play a crucial role in training parents and caregivers to support their child's development and manage challenging behaviors.

In essence, both professionals are integral to the care of children with autism. Psychiatrists bring a medical perspective, including medication management, while psychologists offer psychological expertise, assessment, therapy, and behavioral interventions. Often, a comprehensive approach involves collaboration between these professionals to address the diverse needs of children with autism comprehensively.

Psychological Evaluation

A psychological evaluation is an in-depth assessment conducted by a qualified mental health professional to gain a comprehensive understanding of an individual's psychological functioning. Think of it as a deep dive into a person's mental landscape, using a variety of tools and techniques. It's like piecing together a complex puzzle to get a clear picture of a person's emotional well-being, cognitive abilities, personality traits, and behavioral patterns[84].

In the context of autism, a psychological evaluation plays a crucial role. Because autism varies widely in its manifestations and severity, a psychological evaluation is essential for accurate diagnosis and understanding the individual's specific needs and strengths. Here's what typically happens during a psychological evaluation for autism:

1. Clinical Interview: This involves detailed conversations with the individual and, in the case of children, their parents or caregivers. It's about gathering history, developmental milestones, current functioning, and everyday challenges.

2. Observation: The professional observes the individual's behavior, social interactions, and communication skills in different settings.

3. Testing: This can include a range of standardized tests to assess cognitive abilities, language skills, adaptive functioning, and possible behavioral and emotional issues.

4. Review of Records: The evaluator may review previous medical, educational, or psychological records for additional insights.

As for how often it should be done, this can vary based on individual circumstances. Initially, a psychological evaluation is conducted to aid in the diagnosis of autism. After diagnosis, the frequency of re-evaluation depends on various factors like age, developmental changes, and the emergence of new challenges or symptoms. For children with autism, regular re-evaluations are often recommended to update their educational and therapeutic plans. These evaluations can help track progress, identify emerging issues, and adjust interventions as needed.

A psychological evaluation conducted by a school and one performed by a private practitioner differ in several ways due to variations in scope, purpose, resources, and professional backgrounds. First, a psychological evaluation conducted by a school is typically focused on assessing the child's educational needs and eligibility for special education services under the Individuals with Disabilities

Education Act (IDEA). The evaluation is often conducted by school psychologists or other professionals within the school's special education department. These evaluations primarily aim to identify learning disabilities, developmental delays, or emotional/behavioral issues that may impact the child's academic performance and require educational interventions or accommodations.

Additionally, the tools and resources available for conducting evaluations may differ between school-based and private evaluations. School-based evaluations often rely on standardized assessments that are commonly used in educational settings and may be limited by time constraints and available resources. Private evaluations, on the other hand, may utilize a wider range of assessment tools and techniques, including specialized tests and observations tailored to the individual child's needs. The qualifications and training of the professionals conducting the evaluations may vary. School psychologists are typically trained in educational assessment and interventions within the school system.

Overall, while both school-based and private psychological evaluations serve important purposes, they may differ in scope, depth, and focus. Parents may choose to pursue private evaluations for a more comprehensive understanding of their child's strengths, challenges, and needs, especially if they have concerns beyond academic performance or if they seek specific recommendations for interventions or treatments outside the school setting. However, school-based evaluations remain valuable for assessing educational needs and determining eligibility for special education services within the school system.

NOTES

"Quiet Hands"

The phrase "quiet hands," often employed in some educational or therapeutic contexts, is used to discourage behaviors such as stimming (self-stimulatory behavior) in individuals with autism. This approach, while historically prevalent, has increasingly come under scrutiny for its implications and potential harm.

Stimming is a natural behavior for individuals with autism and includes various repetitive movements or sounds such as hand-flapping, rocking, or humming. These behaviors are not merely habits; they serve crucial functions. Stimming can help individuals manage sensory overload, express emotions, and self-soothe in times of stress or excitement. It is a way for those with autism to maintain equilibrium in their sensory environment and cope with overwhelming external stimuli.

The directive to keep "quiet hands" can be problematic for several reasons. First, it disregards the intrinsic value and purpose of stimming. By compelling an individual to suppress these behaviors, we deny them a fundamental tool for emotional and sensory regulation. This suppression can lead to increased anxiety, stress, and even a sense of shame about their natural inclinations and ways of interacting with the world.

There is a growing movement toward understanding and respecting the needs and behaviors of individuals with autism rather than trying to conform them to typical behavioral standards. This shift emphasizes the importance of accepting stimming as a part of the neurological makeup of a person with autism. Rather than discouraging stimming, the focus has moved to ensuring that these behaviors are safe and appropriate in context, helping individuals find balance between self-expression and social or environmental demands.

In place of discouraging stimming, educators and therapists are encouraged to create supportive environments that respect an individual's need to stim. This involves understanding the triggers and functions of stimming and, when necessary, teaching individuals how to manage their behaviors in ways that are socially acceptable and less disruptive without completely suppressing them.

By moving away from the "quiet hands" directive, we foster an inclusive and understanding atmosphere that respects the neurodiversity of individuals with autism. This approach not only upholds their dignity but also supports their overall well-being and ability to engage with the world on their own terms.

Now, what are some alternatives to using "quiet hands"? The key is to provide options that respect their sensory needs and offer safe, appropriate ways to engage in stimming or other behaviors:

1. Provide Sensory Alternatives: Offer sensory toys or tools that are compatible with hand flapping. For example, toys that can be squeezed and water toys can meet similar sensory needs as the behavior attempting to be replaced.

2. Use Visual Cues: Instead of verbal instructions, use visual cues to guide behavior in a non-intrusive way.

3. Structured Choices: Offer structured choices that allow for movement and sensory exploration in a safe way.

4. Teach Specific Skills: Instead of focusing on what not to do, teach skills that are useful in other ways.

5. Positive Reinforcement: Reinforce desired behaviors with positive feedback and encouragement, focusing on what they are doing right.

6. Model Desired Behavior: Sometimes, showing the desired behavior is more effective than verbal instructions.

7. Create a Safe Environment for Stimming: Ensure there's room for safe stimming behaviors that don't interfere with the activity or safety.

By focusing on respectful, positive approaches that recognize the needs and preferences of individuals with autism, we can create a more inclusive and understanding environment.

Quiet Time

Children with autism often experience the world with heightened sensory sensitivity. The hustle and bustle of everyday life can be overwhelming, like a cacophony of discordant sounds. Quiet and alone time acts as a soothing balm, allowing these children to escape from sensory overload. It's akin to turning down the volume of the world, giving them a chance to process and decompress in a more tranquil setting.

Just as an artist will retreat to find peace and inspiration, children with autism use quiet time to emotionally recalibrate. In the stillness, they find space to navigate their emotions, away from the glare of external stimuli. This time is vital for emotional development and understanding, offering them a canvas to paint their feelings in their own time and pace. In this sanctuary of solitude, children discover and embrace their autonomy. They learn to engage with activities of their choosing, from simple pleasures like flipping through a book to more complex tasks. This autonomy is empowering, instilling a sense of self-reliance and confidence, much like a young bird taking that first tentative flight from the nest. Quiet and alone time isn't just a luxury; it's a fundamental component of their well-being and development. By understanding and providing this precious time, we're not just acknowledging their needs; we're providing space for them to process the world in their own way and in their own time.

R

NOTES

Receptive Language

Receptive language, which encompasses the ability to understand and comprehend spoken or written language, is a fundamental aspect of effective communication and interaction. This linguistic skill involves grasping vocabulary meanings, comprehending sentence structures, active listening, following directions accurately, understanding abstract concepts, and making inferences from language. For children with autism, receptive language holds particular significance. Many individuals on the autism spectrum may experience challenges in developing and utilizing these skills, which can impact their ability to engage meaningfully with others and navigate daily life. Additionally, the ability to infer implied meanings or interpret non-literal language can be challenging, affecting their comprehension of humor, sarcasm, or metaphors[85].

Furthermore, receptive language deficits can impact a child's educational progress and social interactions. For example, understanding abstract concepts, such as time or emotions, may pose difficulties, hindering their ability to relate to peers or excel academically. As a result, tailored interventions and therapies are often employed to enhance receptive language skills in children with autism, empowering them to engage more effectively with the world and those around them.

Registered Behavior Technician (RBT)

A Registered Behavior Technician (RBT) is a professional within the field of Applied Behavior Analysis (ABA) who works directly with individuals with autism and other developmental disabilities[86]. Their primary role involves implementing behavior intervention plans and strategies under the supervision of a Board Certified Behavior Analyst (BCBA) or Board Certified Assistant Behavior Analyst (BCaBA). RBTs work directly with individuals, providing one-on-one therapy sessions where they assist in skill acquisition, such as communication, social interaction, daily living skills, and academic abilities[8].

They also play a major role in behavior reduction, working to decrease challenging behaviors by employing strategies that encourage positive behavior. RBTs collect data during therapy sessions to track progress, ensuring that the skills learned generalize to various settings and real-life situations. Collaboration with BCBAs or BCaBAs is essential, as they regularly review progress, discuss strategies, and make any necessary adjustments to the intervention plan. RBTs follow strict ethical standards and professional conduct guidelines to prioritize the well-being and safety of the individuals they work with, making them a vital part of ABA therapy teams. It is important to note that RBTs cannot work outside of the supervision of a BCBA per the Behavior Analyst Certification Board (BACB) in any setting.

Reinforcement

Reinforcement, in the world of behavior and child development, is a powerful tool that parents and teachers can use to shape behavior in a positive way. It is a process where a specific consequence follows a behavior, making it more likely that the behavior will occur again in the future. Positive reinforcement involves adding something pleasant or desirable after a behavior, with the goal of increasing the likelihood that the behavior will happen again. It's like giving a reward to encourage a specific action[87]. Here's an example:

Imagine a child cleans their room, and you give them a sticker as reward. In this case, the sticker is the positive reinforcement because it's something desirable that's added to encourage the behavior of cleaning the room.

Now, negative reinforcement may sound a bit confusing because it involves removing something unpleasant or aversive after a behavior to increase the likelihood of that behavior happening again. It's like taking away or escaping from something undesirable. Here's an example:

Let's say a child hates doing their homework, and they often procrastinate. You decide that if they complete their homework early, they don't have to do a chore. In this case, not having to do the chore (removing an unpleasant task) is the negative reinforcement to encourage the behavior of doing homework early.

So, how can parents and teachers use reinforcement effectively? Let's get practical:

1. Identify Target Behaviors: First, identify the specific behaviors you want to encourage in your child. Is it finishing their chores, doing homework, or practicing good manners, etc.?

2. Choose the Right Reinforcer: Select a reward that's meaningful. It could be praise, extra playtime, a small treat, or any other positive thing they value.

3. Timing is Key: Deliver the reinforcement immediately after the desired behavior. The closer in time, the stronger the association.

4. Consistency Matters: Be consistent with your reinforcement. If you reward a behavior one day and forget the next, you might create confusion or mistrust.

5. Fade Out Over Time: Once the behavior becomes more consistent, gradually reduce the frequency of reinforcement. You want the behavior to become internalized and not solely reliant on rewards.

6. Communication is Crucial: Talk about the reinforcement system. Explain why it's in place and how they can earn rewards through positive behavior.

7. Monitor Progress: Be mindful of their response to the reinforcement. If something isn't working, be flexible and adjust your approach.

Both types of reinforcement aim to increase the likelihood of a specific behavior occurring in the future, but they do it in different ways – one by adding something good, and the other by taking away something not-so-good. Remember, you can use both positive and negative reinforcement strategies, depending on the situation and the behavior they want to encourage. It's all about finding what works best for your child and the specific context.

Respite Care

Respite care refers to a valuable support service designed to provide temporary relief to families and caregivers who are responsible for individuals with autism[88]. This type of care is essential for families who often face the challenges and demands associated with caring for a child or family member with autism. Respite care offers caregivers a much-needed break from their caregiving responsibilities, allowing them to rest, recharge, and tend to their own well-being.

Autism often involves a range of developmental and behavioral needs that can be intensive and exhausting for caregivers. These needs may include supporting communication difficulties, managing sensory sensitivities, addressing repetitive behaviors, and implementing specialized interventions and therapies. Providing continuous care can be emotionally and physically taxing for caregivers, making respite care an essential service.

Respite care services for individuals with autism are typically delivered by trained professionals who have expertise in understanding and supporting the specific needs of individuals on the autism spectrum. These professionals can provide a safe and nurturing environment for the individual with autism while their primary caregivers take a break. During respite care, the individual may engage in activities tailored to their interests and developmental level, receive support with daily living skills, and benefit from structured routines.

This service can have a positive impact on the well-being of both the individual with autism and their caregivers. For the individual with autism, respite care can provide opportunities for social interaction, skill development, and exposure to new experiences in a supportive environment. It can also reduce stress and anxiety by maintaining consistency and routine during the caregiver's absence.

For parents, respite care offers a crucial opportunity to take care of their own physical and mental health. It allows them to rest, manage their stress levels, and engage in self-care activities. By providing caregivers with temporary relief, respite care can enhance their ability to provide effective and compassionate care in the long run, ultimately benefiting the well-being of the individual with autism as well.

Restricted Interest

Restricted interests, often referred to as "special interests" or "obsessions," are a fundamental characteristic commonly associated with autism. These interests are closely related to autism in several significant ways. First, they are one of the diagnostic criteria for autism spectrum disorder (ASD) according to the DSM-5[89], which is the authoritative diagnostic manual used in psychology and psychiatry. In essence, restricted interests are considered one of the core features of autism, making them integral to the diagnosis and understanding of the condition. This intense concentration on specific topics, hobbies, or activities can be a defining characteristic of autism. The level of dedication and immersion in these interests can be quite remarkable and sets them apart from typical interests.

Restricted interests often manifest in the form of repetitive behaviors, which is another core feature of autism. These repetitive behaviors can be directly linked to the individual's special interests. For instance, someone with a keen interest in collecting certain items may engage in repetitive routines related to their collection. This intertwining of restricted interests with repetitive behaviors further underscores their significance in the autism spectrum.

In the realm of communication and social interaction, restricted interests can also play a pivotal role. Individuals with autism may find it challenging to engage in typical social interactions because their interests tend to be highly specific and intense. Consequently, they may steer conversations toward their special interests, making it difficult to engage in reciprocal and conventional social exchanges. This aspect of restricted interests is closely tied to the broader social communication difficulties often observed in individuals with autism.

These special interests can serve as sources of comfort and predictability for individuals with autism. In a world that may seem unpredictable and overwhelming, engaging in their special interests can provide a sense of security and emotional regulation. These interests act as anchors that help individuals with autism navigate their environment and manage their emotions more effectively.

While restricted interests are a common and defining feature of autism, it's important to recognize that they can vary widely from person to person. These interests are highly individualized and can encompass a wide range of subjects, from academic topics and hobbies to specific activities or collections. They can also evolve over time or persist throughout a person's life, reflecting the diversity of interests and talents within the autism community. Acknowledging and respecting these special interests is essential for understanding and supporting individuals with autism effectively.

Role Play

Role play serves as a highly beneficial and effective tool for aiding in various aspects of development and social skills among children with autism, offering valuable opportunities for practice and mastery within a safe and structured environment[90]. First, role play provides a platform for enhancing social skills, which is a common area of difficulty. Through role play scenarios, both parents and teachers can facilitate practice and learning of social norms such as taking turns, making eye contact, and initiating conversations. For instance, parents can engage in role plays at home, simulating greetings where they take turns saying "hello" and "goodbye" while maintaining eye contact, thereby helping their child become more comfortable with these interactions. Similarly, teachers can orchestrate role plays in the classroom, encouraging students to engage in social interactions with peers in a supportive environment.

Role play also contributes to the improvement of communication skills, which are often challenging for children with autism. By engaging in role play scenarios, both parents and teachers can provide a context for practicing language and encourage children to use words and phrases effectively. Parents can lead role plays at home that simulate common situations, such as ordering food at a restaurant, to assist their child in communicating preferences and needs confidently. Likewise, teachers can facilitate role plays in the classroom, providing students with opportunities to practice communication skills through structured activities.

Role play supports emotional regulation, an area where many children with autism may struggle. By exploring and expressing feelings in a controlled setting, both parents and teachers can help children develop a better understanding of emotions. For example, parents can create role play scenarios at home where their child experiences frustration or anger, providing opportunities to teach coping strategies and appropriate emotional responses. Similarly, teachers can incorporate role plays into classroom activities to address emotions and teach students how to manage them effectively.

Additionally, role play fosters flexibility and problem-solving skills, addressing the rigid thinking patterns often observed in children with autism. Scenarios involving unexpected twists or changes help children learn to adapt and problem-solve creatively. Both parents and teachers can initiate role plays that challenge children to think outside the box and come up with alternative solutions to problems they encounter.

Role play also facilitates the development of generalization skills. By designing scenarios that mimic real-life situations, both parents and teachers help children apply learned skills to various settings. For example, practicing phone conversations during role play sessions at home can transfer to actual phone calls with relatives or friends. Likewise, teachers can create role play activities in the classroom that simulate real-world scenarios, allowing students to generalize skills learned in class to different contexts.

Routines

Routines are an integral part of the lives of individuals with autism, and their relationship with this condition is profound. First and foremost, routines offer individuals with autism a sense of predictability and comfort. In a world that often feels chaotic and overwhelming, adhering to a set routine can create a profound sense of stability and reduce anxiety. Knowing what to expect at specific times of the day can be immensely reassuring for individuals with autism. Knowing that they can rely on their established routines can make the world feel less unpredictable[91].

Routines can enhance focus and attention. Children thrive when they can engage in activities or tasks within a structured routine. The familiarity and predictability of routines can lead to increased productivity and a better ability to concentrate on specific tasks, which can be particularly advantageous in educational and work settings.

Routines can also have implications for communication and social interaction. Some individuals with autism may incorporate routines into their interactions with others. For example, they may use scripts or repetitive phrases as part of their routines to engage in conversation. Routines can serve as a way to initiate or maintain communication for some individuals with autism. However, it's essential to note that while routines offer numerous benefits, they can also lead to resistance to change. Individuals with autism may become particularly distressed when disruptions occur in their established routines. This resistance to change can sometimes result in challenging behaviors. Therefore, it's crucial to find a balance between providing the comfort of routines and allowing for flexibility to adapt to new situations or changes in daily life.

In educational settings, routines are often used to foster learning and classroom management. Many individuals with autism thrive when they have a structured and consistent learning environment. Teachers frequently employ visual schedules and routines to support their students with autism in their learning journey.

It's important to recognize that routines can vary significantly. Some may have highly structured and rigid routines, while others may have more flexible routines that allow for greater adaptability. The degree to which routines are emphasized can differ widely from person to person, highlighting the need for personalized approaches that consider individual preferences and needs.

NOTES

Safety

When discussing the safety of children with autism, both parents and teachers must prioritize and understand the heightened risks involved. A significant concern in this regard is elopement, where startlingly, nearly 50% of these children attempt to elope at least once after the age of four[92]. This behavior can place them in perilous situations, whether it's near busy streets or bodies of water, increasing the likelihood of accidents.

The risk extends to drowning, which remains a leading cause of death among children with autism, particularly following elopement episodes. Many children with autism are drawn to water but may not grasp the potential dangers, such as depth perception and water currents, enhancing the risk of drowning. Furthermore, their sensory perceptions may lead them into other types of hazardous situations, like failing to recognize the danger of a hot stove or an oncoming car.

To mitigate these dangers, a comprehensive and multifaceted safety plan is essential, tailored specifically to each child's needs and the settings they frequent, including home and school. This plan should involve the use of alternative communication methods, such as picture cards or specialized apps, especially for children who face challenges with traditional forms of communication. Additionally, environmental modifications are crucial; for instance, installing alarms on doors and securing pools with fencing can prevent unintended access to hazardous areas.

Ultimately, ensuring the safety of children with autism transcends mere statistics—it requires a profound understanding of their sensory and communication challenges and a commitment to adapt their environments accordingly. This commitment should aim to create a safer, more inclusive world where children with autism can thrive securely and with confidence. Parents and teachers alike should consider what safety initiatives could be implemented locally to better protect these exceptional children and enhance their well-being in the community.

Schedules

The significance of schedules and routines for individuals with autism is profoundly intertwined with their way of interpreting the world. For many with autism, a structured routine is not merely a preference but a vital foundation of stability in what can seem like an overwhelmingly unpredictable environment. For individuals with autism, routines offer a sense of predictability and security, providing comfort in knowing what to expect. This predictability is essential as it can significantly diminish anxiety and stress, which are often exacerbated in unfamiliar settings. With a clear understanding of the day's events, individuals with autism are better prepared mentally and emotionally, gaining a sense of control over their surroundings[93].

Well-structured schedules are instrumental in fostering life skills and independence. Regular routines help establish habits and lessen dependence on caregivers for daily activities. This independence becomes increasingly important as children with autism grow older and seek more autonomy. Through consistent routines, they can master crucial life skills such as personal hygiene, time management, and task prioritization in a manageable and approachable manner.

In educational environments, the benefits of structured routines are particularly pronounced. They contribute to creating a learning atmosphere where individuals with autism can excel. Predictable schedules enhance focus, improve engagement with educational materials, and minimize the likelihood of disruptive behaviors that may arise from uncertainty or sensory overload. However, it's vital to balance the security provided by a consistent schedule with the flexibility to handle life's inherent unpredictability. Gradually introducing small changes can help individuals with autism adapt, ensuring they feel safe and supported as they learn to manage new situations[94].

Parents can utilize schedules at home by maintaining consistent daily routines, such as regular meal times, bedtime routines, and structured playtimes. Visual schedules can be especially helpful, allowing children to see what activities are planned and when transitions will occur. Teachers, on the other hand, can implement schedules in the classroom by starting each day with a clear outline of the day's activities. Using visual aids such as charts or boards to indicate the schedule can help students know what to expect and when changes might occur. Consistency in classroom management and routine activities can significantly aid in reducing classroom disruptions and enhancing the learning experience.

Scripting

Scripting is a behavior commonly observed in children with autism, and there are several reasons why they might engage in this activity. It involves repeating or echoing words, phrases, or even whole dialogues, often from TV shows, movies, books, or conversations[95]. This behavior is known as "scripting" because the child is essentially reciting a "script" they've heard elsewhere. Scripting can serve as a method of communication. Some children may use scripted phrases borrowed from familiar sources, such as movies or books, to express their feelings or needs. This can be especially useful for those who find it difficult to formulate their own words.

Additionally, scripting offers comfort and a way to cope with stress. The familiarity and predictability of repeating known phrases provide a soothing effect, particularly in overwhelming or stressful situations. It can also act as a form of stimulatory behavior, commonly known as stimming. This helps in self-soothing and managing sensory input, which is beneficial for children experiencing sensory overload or anxiety[96].

When a child engages in scripting, it's important to understand and appropriately respond to this behavior. Scripting, or the repetitive recitation of words or phrases, can be a significant communication tool for children with autism. It might serve various functions such as expressing needs, coping with anxiety, or simply enjoying the rhythm and familiarity of the repeated words.

The first step in responding to scripting is to discern why the child is scripting. Is it a method for communication, a response to stress, or a form of self-soothing during overstimulation? Understanding these triggers is crucial as it informs how adults should react and support the child. Observing when and where scripting occurs can provide insights into its purpose and help in developing effective strategies to support the child.

Engaging with a child's scripting can be a beneficial strategy. For instance, if a child frequently scripts lines from a favorite show, parents and teachers can use these scripts as a bridge to more interactive communication. By responding to the scripted lines or asking questions about them, adults can turn a solitary activity into an opportunity for engagement and connection.

Both at home and in the classroom, encouraging a child to expand beyond scripting into more spontaneous communication is valuable. This can be achieved by modeling new phrases or creating scenarios where the child might feel motivated to try new expressions or modify their usual scripts. The key is to ensure that these opportunities are presented in a supportive, low-pressure environment, allowing the child to explore communication without stress.

It's essential that both home and school environments are structured to make the child feel safe and supported. This includes accepting the child's need to script without judgment, providing a predictable routine that reduces anxiety, and patiently supporting the child's developmental journey. Consistency between home and school settings can make the child feel more secure and support continuous progress[97].

If concerns arise about the impact of scripting on the child's ability to interact or learn effectively, or if the behavior significantly interferes with daily activities, it may be beneficial to consult with professionals. Speech therapists or autism specialists can offer personalized strategies that are tailored to the child's specific needs, helping to integrate more functional communication skills while respecting the child's natural tendencies.

Remember, scripting is an aspect of how some children with autism interact with the world. By understanding, accepting, and thoughtfully responding to scripting, both parents and teachers can play a pivotal role in helping the child navigate their environment more effectively and confidently. Embracing this aspect of the child's behavior with empathy and informed strategies is necessary for their growth and well-being.

Self Advocate

A self-advocate is someone who actively speaks up for and represents their own interests, needs, and rights. The individual's role as a self advocate is especially vital in the autism community. It gives individuals with autism a powerful voice in conversations and decisions impacting their lives. The significance of listening to self-advocates cannot be overstated.

First and foremost, self-advocates offer an invaluable perspective through their first-hand experiences with autism. Their personal insights provide a deeper understanding of what it means to live with autism, which is crucial for parents, educators, therapists, and policy makers. These narratives help in breaking down stereotypes and misconceptions about autism, fostering greater awareness and understanding within the broader community[98].

By actively participating in dialogues about autism, self-advocates ensure they are fairly and accurately represented. This empowerment is key in ensuring their needs and rights are considered and respected. They play a pivotal role in advocating for the rights of individuals with autism, promoting greater inclusivity, accessibility, and equality in various spheres of society[99]. Listening to self-advocates is not just about giving them a platform; it's about genuinely comprehending and incorporating their experiences and needs into the larger conversation about autism. Their voices are essential in shaping a more inclusive and empathetic world, where the diversity of the autism spectrum is recognized, valued, and celebrated.

Self-Contained Classroom

A self-contained classroom is a specialized educational setting designed for students who require intensive and individualized instructional support. Typically, these classrooms cater to students with significant learning differences, disabilities, or special needs that cannot be adequately addressed in a general education setting. The students who need this placement often include those with profound learning disabilities, severe autism, emotional and behavioral disorders, or other conditions that demand a high level of specialized attention and resources[100].

One of the primary advantages of a self-contained classroom is the tailored instruction it provides. With smaller class sizes and a higher teacher-to-student ratio, these classrooms offer personalized education plans that cater to each student's learning style and needs. The environment is generally more structured and predictable, which can be beneficial for students who struggle with the stimuli and variances of a regular classroom setting. Self-contained classrooms are equipped with specialized resources and staff trained to handle specific disabilities, while providing a supportive and understanding learning environment[101].

However, there are also drawbacks to consider. One significant concern is the potential for social isolation. Students in self-contained classrooms may have fewer opportunities to interact with their peers in the general education setting, which can impact their social development and integration skills. Additionally, there's a risk of stigmatization, as being separated from the mainstream student body can sometimes lead to feelings of being 'different' or 'othered'[102].

Another con is the possible limitation in the breadth of the curriculum. While these classrooms focus on personalized and functional skills, they may not always offer the same academic rigor or variety of subjects found in general education settings. This can sometimes lead to gaps in a student's overall education or limit their exposure to diverse learning experiences.

It's important to weigh the benefits of individualized attention and specialized resources against the potential drawbacks of social isolation and curricular limitations. Striking a balance and ensuring that students have opportunities for inclusion and interaction with the broader school community can help mitigate some of these concerns.

Sensory Integration Therapy

Sensory Integration Therapy is a therapeutic approach designed to help people, particularly children who have sensory processing issues. This kind of therapy is often used for individuals with autism, attention deficit hyperactivity disorder (ADHD), and other developmental conditions, although its application can be broader.

The core idea behind Sensory Integration Therapy is that by improving the way the brain processes sensory information, individuals can respond more effectively to their environment. Sensory processing issues can make it difficult for some people to interpret and respond to information from their senses. For instance, they might find certain textures unbearable, have difficulty coping with bright lights or loud noises, or struggle with spatial and bodily awareness[103].

Sensory Integration Therapy typically involves engaging in activities that are structured to challenge a person's ability to respond to sensory input. This is done in a controlled and gradual manner. The activities are designed to be playful and enjoyable, to keep the individual engaged. They might include swinging, playing in a ball pit, handling materials with various textures, or balance activities.

The therapy aims to help the individual adapt to sensory experiences, learn how to modulate their responses, and integrate sensory information more effectively. For example, a child who is hypersensitive to touch might be gradually exposed to different textures in a non-threatening way, helping them become more comfortable with a variety of tactile sensations.

The benefits of Sensory Integration Therapy can include improved motor skills, better coordination, increased awareness of the environment, and a reduction in problems associated with sensory processing, such as anxiety or behavioral issues[104]. It's important to note that while Sensory Integration Therapy can be beneficial for many, it's not a one-size-fits-all solution. The effectiveness can vary depending on the individual's needs and the specific challenges they face with sensory processing. It's typically recommended as part of a broader therapeutic approach, tailored to the individual's needs.

Sensory Systems

Understanding the seven, yes seven, sensory systems is crucial in appreciating how individuals with autism perceive and interact with the world around them. Each system can present either hypersensitivity (over-responsiveness) or hyposensitivity (under-responsiveness), creating unique sensory experiences for each person[105].

Visual System (Vision): The visual system processes what we see. Those who are hypersensitive may find bright lights or certain color patterns overwhelming, leading to discomfort or even pain. On the flip side, individuals who are hyposensitive may need more visual stimuli to engage their attention, potentially overlooking subtle visual cues. To cater to these sensitivities, activities like using dimmed lighting or color filters can help the hypersensitive, while visually stimulating activities like puzzles or light tables can engage the hyposensitive.

Auditory System (Hearing): This system is all about how we hear. Hypersensitive individuals might find everyday sounds like a vacuum cleaner or phone ringing excessively loud and distressing. Conversely, those who are hyposensitive may not react to sounds that others notice, or they might seek out loud, noisy environments. Noise-canceling headphones can be a sanctuary for the hypersensitive, while music therapy or sound-based games can provide appropriate stimulation for those who are hyposensitive.

Olfactory System (Smell): The sense of smell can be a source of discomfort for those who are hypersensitive, where even pleasant smells might be overpowering. Those with hyposensitivity might not react to strong odors or might seek them out. Maintaining a neutral-smelling environment can help hypersensitive individuals, whereas scent matching games can be stimulating for those who are hyposensitive.

Gustatory System (Taste): Taste sensitivities can greatly affect eating habits. A hypersensitive individual may have a restricted diet, finding certain flavors too intense. In contrast, a hyposensitive person might prefer very spicy or strong flavors, or they may chew or suck on non-food items. Introducing new foods slowly and in a controlled manner can help those who are hypersensitive, while offering a variety of strong-flavored foods can cater to those who are hyposensitive.

Tactile System (Touch): This system deals with how we perceive touch. Hypersensitivity can manifest as discomfort with certain clothing textures or an aversion to physical touch. Hyposensitivity, however, may lead to a lack of response to pain or a desire for strong pressure or textures. Solutions like soft, seamless clothing can comfort the hypersensitive, while sensory bins or weighted blankets can satisfy the tactile needs of the hyposensitive.

Vestibular System (Balance/Movement): The vestibular system is key to our sense of balance and spatial orientation. Those hypersensitive to vestibular input may become dizzy or nauseated with movements like swinging or spinning. On the other end, hyposensitive individuals may crave such movements, showing an ability to tolerate, or even enjoy, intense spinning or rocking without getting dizzy. Gentle rocking or balancing activities can be helpful for the hypersensitive, while playground swings or spinning activities can be beneficial for those seeking more intense vestibular input.

Proprioceptive System (Body Position and Movement): This system helps us understand our body's position and movement in space. Hypersensitivity might lead to a sense of clumsiness or a difficulty in gauging strength during activities. In contrast, those with hyposensitivity might seek deep pressure, have trouble with personal space, or enjoy heavy physical activities. For the hypersensitive, light exercise or yoga can be beneficial, while activities like jumping on a trampoline or carrying heavy objects might satisfy the proprioceptive needs of the hyposensitive.

Each of these sensory systems plays a vital role in how individuals with autism interact with the world. Tailoring environments and activities to their specific sensory needs can significantly improve their comfort, engagement, and overall quality of life. Understanding and respecting these sensory differences is key to supporting individuals with autism in a sensitive and effective manner[106].

Occupational therapists (OTs) are instrumental in assisting individuals with sensory processing challenges, often observed in autism and related developmental conditions. They start by conducting a thorough assessment to understand how an individual responds to sensory stimuli, identifying patterns of hypersensitivity, hyposensitivity, or sensory seeking behaviors. Based on this assessment, OTs create personalized 'sensory diets'— specific activities tailored to provide the necessary sensory input to help an individual stay focused and organized. They also play a key role in modifying environments, making them more sensory-friendly, and in developing essential coping and self-regulation skills to manage sensory overload. This might include recommending sensory tools like weighted blankets or noise-cancelling headphones. Educating parents, teachers, and caregivers is another crucial aspect of their work, ensuring consistent support across different environments. OTs employ sensory integration therapy to help individuals process sensory information more effectively and focus on everyday living skills, making daily tasks less overwhelming. Additionally, they promote the development of social and play skills, taking sensory preferences and challenges into consideration to improve the individual's overall function and participation in daily life[107].

Service Animal

Service animals, particularly dogs, play a transformative role in the lives of individuals with autism, offering support in a myriad of ways. These animals are trained specifically to assist with the challenges that people on the autism spectrum may face. The benefits of a service animal are multifaceted. Primarily these animals provide a calming presence which can be incredibly beneficial for individuals who experience sensory overloads or frequent meltdowns. The consistent companionship of a service animal can reduce anxiety and stress, offering a sense of security and routine. Furthermore, service animals can be trained to intervene in situations where the individual may be at risk, such as preventing them from running into traffic or guiding them away from potentially harmful behaviors. They can also assist in developing social skills by increasing opportunities for social interactions, as the animal can act as a social bridge, making it easier for individuals with autism to engage with others[108].

However, there are also considerations and challenges to think about. The cost of acquiring and maintaining a service animal can be significant, including expenses for training, healthcare, food, and other supplies. There's also the commitment of time and energy to ensure the animal is properly cared for. Additionally, having a service animal requires a certain level of public interaction, which might not be comfortable for all individuals with autism, given the likelihood of people approaching to inquire about the animal.

In terms of expected outcomes, while a service animal can provide remarkable support and improvements in quality of life, it's important to have realistic expectations. The animal can offer companionship, reduce anxiety, and assist in daily routines, but it's not a cure for autism nor will it eliminate all challenges associated with the condition[109].

For those considering getting a service animal, the process involves several steps. Before making the decision, it's important to assess whether a service animal is the right fit for the individual's needs and lifestyle. Consulting with healthcare providers or therapists who understand the individual's specific challenges with autism is a good starting point. Once the decision is made, the next step is to find a reputable organization that trains service animals for people with autism. These organizations often have specific processes for matching a service animal to an individual's needs. It's crucial to ensure the organization is legitimate and follows ethical practices in training and handling animals. The training process is rigorous and can take a considerable amount of time, as the animal needs to be trained to cater to specific needs and behaviors. Lastly, there's also the aspect of legal rights and understanding where service animals are allowed, which varies by region and country.

Social Skills

Social skills are critical for effective communication and interaction, encompassing both verbal and non-verbal abilities like speech, gestures, facial expressions, and body language. Mastering these skills often poses significant challenges, resulting in various social deficits. One of the primary challenges some children with autism face is difficulty in understanding and interpreting social cues. They may struggle with non-verbal signals such as facial expressions, body language, and eye contact, which makes it difficult for them to read others' emotions or intentions. Communication issues are also common; these children might have a limited vocabulary, speak in a monotone, or find initiating and maintaining conversations challenging. They often find it hard to grasp the unwritten rules of social interaction, like turn-taking or respecting personal space, and their tendency to interpret language literally can lead to misunderstandings. Additionally, some might show limited interest in social interactions, preferring solitary activities over engaging with peers[110].

Both parents and teachers play crucial roles in developing necessary social skills. Parents can model appropriate social behaviors at home, demonstrating actions like making eye contact, using polite language, and showing empathy, providing clear examples for their children to emulate. Similarly, teachers can reinforce these behaviors in the classroom and provide structured social interaction exercises. Social stories and role-playing are valuable tools. These methods help children understand and practice social interactions, preparing them for various social situations they might encounter.

In addition, encouraging participation in structured settings, such as classes or clubs aligned with their interests, offers controlled environments and interactions that are less likely to be overwhelming for children with autism. Positive social behaviors should be praised and reinforced, encouraging further engagement. Visual aids and supports are also beneficial, particularly for children who respond well to visual stimuli. Both at home and in school, using tools like emotion cards or social situation flashcards can aid in teaching these critical skills.

Social Stories

Social stories are an innovative and practical tool, originally developed for individuals with autism, to help them navigate complex social situations. Conceived by Carol Gray in the 1990s[111], these are short, carefully crafted narratives that aim to convey information about a particular social situation, event, or activity, and include guidance on appropriate responses or behaviors. Tailored to the individual's perspective and understanding, these stories break down social scenarios into understandable and manageable components.

The structure of social stories typically involves several key elements. Descriptive sentences set the context, detailing where and when the situation occurs, who is involved, and what actions are taking place. Directive sentences provide gentle guidance on expected behaviors or responses in the situation. Additionally, perspective sentences are crucial as they shed light on the reactions and feelings of others involved. This aspect is particularly beneficial for fostering empathy and perspective-taking, helping the reader to understand how their actions might affect others.

The benefits of using social stories are multifaceted. One benefit is they significantly aid in improving an individual's comprehension of social situations, which can often be challenging for those with ASD. By clarifying what is expected in a given scenario, social stories can alleviate anxiety and stress, especially in new or unfamiliar settings. They are also instrumental in enhancing communication skills, providing examples of appropriate dialogue and behavior in social interactions[112].

Social stories are effective in promoting behavioral change and adaptation. They can be used to introduce and reinforce new behaviors or to prepare for changes in routine, offering a consistent and clear message about the desired outcomes. Over time, this can lead to increased independence, as individuals develop the skills and confidence to handle social situations on their own.

For optimal effectiveness, social stories should be personalized and directly relevant to the individual's experiences. Writing them in a positive tone and focusing on appropriate behaviors and responses is key. Additionally, incorporating pictures or other visual aids can be extremely helpful, particularly for visual learners. In essence, social stories are a valuable and versatile tool, providing individuals with autism a means to better understand, navigate, and engage with the social world around them.

To further assist in social skill development, parents and teachers can collaborate to create social stories. Here's how:

1. Identify the Purpose: Determine what social situation or skill the social story will address.

2. Write in the First Person: Use the first person point of view to make the story relatable to the child

3. Keep it Simple and Concrete: Use clear and concise language appropriate for the child's understanding level.

4. Incorporate Descriptive, Perspective, and Directive Sentences:
- Descriptive sentences provide basic information about the social situation.
- Perspective sentences describe the internal states of others, such as thoughts and feelings.
- Directive sentences suggest the appropriate responses or behaviors in the given situation.

5. Use Visuals: Include pictures or illustrations that relate to the text to help the child better understand the story.

6. Review and Revise: Once the story is complete, review it to ensure it is accurate and comprehensible. Make any necessary adjustments.

7. Read Regularly: Integrate the social story into the child's daily routine to reinforce learning.

Improving social skills in children with autism is a gradual process that requires patience and persistence. It's essential to celebrate every small step forward and tailor strategies to each child's needs and learning pace.

Special Education

Special education is a branch of education that specifically caters to the needs of students with disabilities. These disabilities can range from learning disabilities and developmental delays to physical disabilities and emotional disturbances. The goal of special education is to provide these students with individualized instruction and resources that address their needs, thereby helping them achieve a higher level of personal self-sufficiency and success in school and their community. There are various types of special education classrooms, each designed to cater to different needs:

1. Self-Contained Classrooms: These are specialized classrooms where students with similar educational needs are grouped together. The curriculum in a self-contained classroom is typically modified to meet the specific needs of the students. The teacher-to-student ratio is usually lower than in a general education classroom, allowing for more individualized attention.

2. Inclusion Classrooms: In inclusion settings, students with disabilities are integrated into general education classrooms. In these environments, special education teachers work alongside general education teachers to modify the curriculum and provide support to meet the individual needs of students with disabilities. This model promotes social integration and inclusion.

3. Classrooms for Intellectual Disabilities: These classrooms are specifically designed for students with intellectual disabilities. The curriculum in these classrooms is often focused on developing life skills and basic literacy and numeracy skills, tailored to the students' cognitive

abilities. The emphasis is on practical, hands-on learning and may include skills for independent living, social skills training, and vocational skills. The teaching is highly individualized, with a strong emphasis on achieving personal independence and self-care skills.

4. Autism-Specific Classrooms: Classrooms designed specifically for students with autism provide a structured environment that addresses the learning needs associated with autism spectrum disorders. These might include:

Structured Teaching: Based on approaches like the TEACCH (Treatment and Education of Autistic and related Communication-handicapped Children) model, these classrooms often feature structured teaching methods with clear physical and visual boundaries.

Sensory-Friendly Environments: These classrooms may have features or resources to address sensory sensitivities, such as sensory rooms, quiet areas, or specific sensory materials (like fidget toys).

Communication Support: Emphasis on communication skills, including the use of augmentative and alternative communication (AAC) systems for non-verbal students or those with limited verbal abilities.

Behavioral Interventions: Use of strategies to manage and support positive behaviors, often incorporating techniques from Applied Behavior Analysis (ABA).

Social Skills Development: Focused instruction on social skills, often using structured social skills programs and opportunities for guided interaction with peers.

5. Multi-Disability Classrooms: These classrooms serve students who have multiple disabilities, which may include a combination of physical, cognitive, sensory, and medical disabilities. The teaching in these classrooms is highly specialized and individualized, focusing on the combination of needs of each student.

6. Resource Rooms: Resource rooms provide support for students with disabilities who spend most of their day in a general education classroom. These students might visit the resource room for a portion of the day to receive more intensive instruction in certain areas, such as reading or math.

7. Pull-Out Classes: Similar to resource rooms, pull-out classes are where students are removed from the general education classroom for part of the day to receive more focused, intensive instruction in a smaller group setting.

8. Integrated Co-Teaching (ICT) Classrooms: In this setting, a general education teacher and a special education teacher work together in the same classroom. The student body in these classrooms includes both general education students and students with disabilities, providing an inclusive environment with access to the general education curriculum, but with the necessary supports and modifications.

9. Therapeutic Classrooms: These are specialized classrooms designed to meet the needs of students with significant emotional, behavioral, or mental health challenges. The focus is on providing a structured environment that includes therapeutic support alongside academic instruction.

Each type of special education classroom is designed to meet different needs and provides varying levels of support. The choice of classroom depends on the individual's educational needs and goals as outlined in their Individualized Education Program (IEP).

Spectrum

When people say that autism is a spectrum, they're referring to the wide range of symptoms, skills, and levels of disability that can occur in individuals with autism. This concept is crucial in understanding the diversity and individuality within the autism community. The term "spectrum" in this context signifies that each person with autism has a distinct set of challenges and strengths. The manifestation of autism varies greatly from one individual to another.

Variations in the spectrum cover a wide range of symptoms. For instance, some individuals with autism might have difficulty with social interactions and communication, ranging from challenges in understanding body language and facial expressions to difficulties in developing and maintaining conversations. Others might exhibit repetitive behaviors or have very focused interests. Sensory sensitivities are also common, where some might be hypersensitive to sensory stimuli like light or sound, while others might be under-responsive.

The concept of the autism spectrum also emphasizes that the level of support needed can change over time, especially with interventions, education, and support. This understanding of autism as a spectrum is essential for providing appropriate and individualized care, education, and support to each person with ASD, acknowledging their abilities and challenges. It challenges the one-size-fits-all view of autism and highlights the need for a personalized approach to each individual's needs.

Speech Therapy

Speech therapy is an essential therapeutic approach that targets improving communication abilities, and it holds particular significance for individuals with autism. This form of therapy addresses a wide range of communication skills, not just limited to speech, but also encompassing overall effective communication. One key area of focus in speech therapy for autism is articulation skills. This involves working on the clarity of speech, as some individuals with autism may struggle with pronouncing words correctly. The therapy aims to enhance these articulation skills, making speech clearer and more understandable. Expressive language skills are also a crucial part of speech therapy. This includes the ability to use words, sentences, gestures, or even writing to express thoughts, needs, and desires. Since expressing themselves can be challenging for those with autism, speech therapy seeks to develop these essential skills[113].

Another important aspect is receptive language skills, which refer to understanding and processing what others say. Speech therapists work to improve listening skills and comprehension of language in individuals with autism. Additionally, social communication skills are often a focus area. Many with autism find navigating the social aspects of language challenging, such as understanding conversational rules, turn-taking, maintaining topics, interpreting humor, and non-literal language. Speech therapy aids in developing these social communication abilities.

Non-verbal communication is also addressed in speech therapy. Effective communication is not just about words; it also involves eye contact, facial expressions, and body language. Speech therapists often help individuals with autism enhance these non-verbal communication skills. For those who are non-verbal or have severe speech limitations, speech therapists might introduce Alternative and Augmentative Communication (AAC) methods. These can range from picture communication boards and sign language to advanced electronic communication devices, providing alternative means for effective communication.

In some cases, speech therapy may also cover feeding and swallowing issues, as the muscles used for swallowing overlap with those used for speech. Some individuals with autism experience difficulties with eating, often related to sensory sensitivities or motor skills challenges. Speech therapists can offer strategies and exercises to address these issues[114].

Speech therapy as a related service in schools is integral to supporting students with communication challenges, such as those with autism, speech delays, or other language impairments. This type of therapy is designed to ensure that students can effectively participate in classroom activities, interact with their peers and teachers, and meet the educational standards outlined in their Individualized Education Programs (IEPs). Its main goal is to remove learning barriers caused by communication issues, thereby enhancing the student's overall educational experience.

In the school setting, speech therapy is tightly integrated with a student's educational objectives. Speech therapists collaborate with educational staff to identify how communication difficulties might be impacting a student's academic performance. For instance, a student struggling with expressive language might find it difficult to participate in class discussions, respond to questions, or complete written tasks. To address these issues, speech therapists develop specific intervention strategies that are implemented within the school curriculum, tailoring their approach to the needs of each student.

Services provided in schools include comprehensive assessments to evaluate a student's speech and language capabilities relative to their peers, individual or group therapy sessions based on the student's needs and IEP goals, and the development of intervention strategies. Speech therapists also consult with teachers to help them implement communication-facilitating strategies in the classroom. Additionally, they are involved in monitoring and adjusting IEP goals to reflect the student's progress and evolving needs.

The collaborative nature of this service is crucial. Speech therapists work closely with a multidisciplinary team that includes teachers, special education professionals, psychologists, and parents. This provides accountability so that speech therapy strategies are consistently applied across all aspects of the student's educational environment, promoting a comprehensive approach to learning and social integration.

It is important to note that, as a related service under the Individuals with Disabilities Education Act (IDEA), speech therapy in schools is provided at no cost to families. It fulfills part of the public education system's obligation to provide a Free Appropriate Public Education (FAPE) to students with disabilities, making essential therapy services accessible to those who might not afford private therapy.

Speech therapy in educational settings plays a fundamental role in helping students with communication impairments to thrive academically and socially. By addressing specific communication challenges in conjunction with educational goals, speech therapists help students fully engage in their education and achieve their academic and social potential.

Stereotyped Behavior (Stereotypy)/ Stimming

Stereotypy, or stereotypic behavior, refers to repetitive, ritualistic actions that are commonly observed in individuals with autism and other developmental disorders[115]. These behaviors are characterized by their repetitive nature and often appear to serve no obvious purpose. Common examples of stereotypic behaviors include hand-flapping, rocking back and forth, spinning objects, echolalia (repeating sounds or phrases), and lining up toys or objects.

The reasons behind stereotypic behaviors can vary and are often complex. Here are some of the key factors that contribute to the occurrence of stereotypy:

1. Sensory Regulation: Many individuals with autism have sensory processing differences. Stereotypic behaviors may help them regulate sensory input. For example, someone who is hypersensitive to sensory stimuli might engage in repetitive behaviors to create a sense of predictability and control in their environment. Conversely, someone who is hyposensitive may use these behaviors to stimulate their senses.

2. Coping Mechanism: Stereotypy can be a way to manage anxiety or stress. Engaging in these repetitive behaviors can provide comfort, relaxation, and a way to cope with overwhelming situations or environments.

3. Communication: Sometimes, stereotypic behaviors are a form of non-verbal communication. An individual with autism might use a repetitive behavior to express excitement, frustration, or other emotions, especially if they have difficulty with traditional forms of communication.

4. Neurological Factors: Research suggests that there may be neurological underpinnings to these behaviors. The brain's reward system, motor pathways, and neural circuits related to habit formation may all play a role in the development and persistence of stereotypic behaviors.

5. Habit Formation: Over time, these behaviors can become habitual. What may start as a response to a sensory need or a coping mechanism can evolve into a regular habit that the individual engages in without conscious thought.

It's important to note that while stereotypic behaviors are common in individuals with autism, they are not exclusive to this group and can be seen in other populations as well. Understanding the function of these behaviors for each individual is key to providing appropriate support and intervention. In some cases, intervention may be necessary, especially if the behavior is harmful or interferes significantly with daily functioning. However, in many instances, these behaviors are as harmless as twirling hair or tapping feet[116].

Strengths

Highlighting a child with autism's strengths is crucial for several reasons with each contributing to the child's overall development, self-esteem, and sense of belonging. First, focusing on strengths helps build self-esteem and confidence. Children with autism, like all individuals, flourish when their talents and abilities are recognized and celebrated. This positive reinforcement encourages them to pursue their interests and passions, contributing to a stronger sense of self-worth. When children see themselves as capable and talented in certain areas, it can counteract any negative feelings or stigma they may experience in other aspects of their lives, particularly in areas where they face challenges.

Emphasizing strengths can lead to better engagement and motivation in learning. Children are naturally more inclined to engage in activities that they are good at and enjoy. By identifying and nurturing these areas, whether it's a skill in a particular academic subject, a creative talent, or a knack for understanding technology, parents and educators can create learning experiences that are both meaningful and enjoyable. This not only makes education more effective but also more enjoyable for the child, fostering a lifelong love of learning.

Additionally, focusing on strengths can offer a more balanced perspective. Children with autism often face a lot of focus on their challenges and the areas where they need support. While addressing these areas is important, an overemphasis can lead to a skewed perception of the child's abilities and potential. Celebrating their strengths provides a more holistic view of the child, acknowledging that despite their challenges, they have much to offer.

NOTES

Tantrum

Understanding the distinction between tantrums and meltdowns is integral when supporting children, especially those with autism. Tantrums typically arise when a child is striving to obtain something they desire or avoid something they dislike. These outbursts often manifest as crying, yelling, and sometimes even physical actions like hitting or object-throwing. They are usually fueled by frustration or a desire for attention[117].

Conversely, meltdowns are more intense and are usually triggered by sensory overload or emotional overwhelm. During a meltdown, a child can completely lose control, becoming inconsolable and sometimes engaging in self-injurious behaviors. It's vital to understand that meltdowns are not a means of manipulation; they are a genuine response to overwhelming stimuli.

Being able to distinguish between the two is important because your response to a tantrum and a meltdown will likely differ. Meltdowns require a little more compassion, while tantrums may require behavior intervention plans. Regardless of the situation, both parents and teachers will need patience and a calm demeanor. For tantrums, maintaining boundaries, offering choices, or using distractions can be effective strategies. However, during meltdowns, it may be necessary to avoid making demands, instead, offer comfort and provide time and space to allow for self-regulation[118].

By recognizing these distinctions, both parents and teachers can effectively navigate the challenges of supporting children with empathy and care. This understanding fosters a supportive environment where children feel understood, valued, and empowered to manage their emotions in healthy ways. Together, as a unified team, parents and teachers can provide the essential support needed for children to thrive and succeed.

Teamwork

Effective collaboration between home and school is central for providing consistent, comprehensive support that addresses the child's needs across different settings. Maintaining open lines of communication is fundamental. Parents and teachers should regularly share information about the child's progress, challenges, and any changes in behavior or routines. This communication can take various forms, including emails, phone calls, notes, or face-to-face meetings. Both parties should feel comfortable reaching out to discuss concerns or share insights, fostering a collaborative approach to supporting the child.

Collaborative planning involves setting shared goals and developing strategies to support the child's academic, social, and emotional development. Parents and teachers should work together to create Individualized Education Programs (IEPs) that reflect the child's strengths, needs, and preferences. This collaborative process ensures that interventions and supports are tailored to the child's individual profile and that everyone is aligned in working towards common objectives.

Both parents and teachers should actively listen to each other's perspectives and insights. Each party brings valuable knowledge and experiences to the table, and by listening attentively, they can gain a deeper understanding of the child's needs and preferences. Active listening fosters mutual respect and trust, laying the foundation for effective collaboration and problem-solving.

Sharing important information between home and school is necessary for maintaining consistency and continuity in the child's support system. Parents can provide insights into the child's interests, routines, and any significant events or changes at home that may impact their behavior or well-being. Likewise, teachers can share updates on the child's progress, academic goals, and any observations made in the classroom. This exchange of information enables both parties to make informed decisions and adjustments to support the child effectively.

Consistency is key when implementing behavior plans and academic goals. Parents and teachers should strive to maintain consistency between home and school environments, upholding strategies and expectations so they remain consistent across different settings. This consistency provides predictability for the child, which is especially important for individuals with autism who thrive on routine and structure. Collaboratively developing and implementing behavior plans, visual supports, and reinforcement strategies can help reinforce consistency and support the child's success across settings.

By working together as a team, parents and teachers can create a supportive and cohesive environment that maximizes the child's potential for growth and success. This collaborative approach fosters a sense of shared responsibility and partnership in meeting the child's needs, ultimately enhancing their overall well-being and development. Together, parents and teachers play a vital role in supporting children with autism on their journey to reaching their full potential.

Transition Goals

Transition goals in an IEP are specific objectives tailored to a student's needs and abilities. They are designed to guide the student's preparation for life after graduation, whether that involves pursuing higher education, entering the workforce, or acquiring independent living skills. These goals encompass various areas, including vocational skills, education, employment, and daily living skills. By outlining tangible objectives, transition goals empower students to work towards their aspirations and become active participants in shaping their future[119].

Transition goals should help facilitate the smooth transition from school to adulthood. They equip students with the skills and knowledge needed to navigate the challenges of post-school life successfully. This transition period can be especially daunting for individuals with disabilities, making these goals even more significant.

Furthermore, transition goals promote self-advocacy and self-determination. They encourage students to voice their preferences, set personal goals, and actively engage in planning their future. This self-awareness and self-advocacy are invaluable skills that empower individuals to make informed decisions.

Implementing transition goals in an IEP involves a collaborative effort among teachers, students, parents, and, in some cases, external support professionals. Here's how they can be effectively implemented:

1. Assessment and Planning: The process begins with a comprehensive assessment of the student's strengths, weaknesses, interests, and aspirations. This assessment forms the basis for developing tailored transition goals. The

IEP team, which includes teachers, parents, and the student, collaborates to set meaningful and achievable objectives.

2. Setting Clear Objectives: Transition goals should be specific, measurable, achievable, relevant, and time-bound (SMART). They should outline what skills or knowledge the student needs to acquire by the end of each school year to progress towards their post-school goals.

3. Individualized Support: Provide individualized support and services that align with the transition goals. This may involve specialized instruction, vocational training, counseling, or access to assistive technology.

4. Regular Review and Monitoring: Transition goals should be regularly reviewed and monitored to track progress. The IEP team should meet periodically to assess whether adjustments or additional supports are needed.

5. Community Involvement: Encourage community involvement, such as internships, job shadowing, or volunteer opportunities, to provide real-world experiences that align with the student's post-school goals.

Trust

Building trust with is of utmost importance in fostering positive relationships and supporting overall well-being and development. Trust forms the foundation for effective communication, learning, and social interaction. Here's why building trust is crucial:

1. Establishing a Safe Environment: Children with autism often thrive in environments that feel safe and predictable. By building trust, educators and caregivers

create a sense of security for the child, allowing them to feel more comfortable and at ease in their surroundings. A safe environment encourages exploration, learning, and social engagement, contributing to the child's overall development.

2. Facilitating Communication: Trust is essential for effective communication with children with autism. When a child trusts their caregivers and educators, they are more likely to communicate their needs, preferences, and emotions openly. This communication enables adults to better understand the child's perspective and provide appropriate support and interventions. Trusting relationships also foster reciprocal communication, where the child feels listened to and respected, leading to improved social interactions and self-expression.

3. Supporting Emotional Regulation: Children with autism may experience challenges with emotional regulation. Building trust with caregivers and educators provides children with a supportive framework for managing their emotions. When a child trusts their caregivers, they are more likely to seek comfort and support during times of distress or overwhelm. This support helps the child develop coping strategies and resilience, ultimately promoting emotional well-being.

4. Promoting Social Connection: Trust is also necessary for fostering social connections and relationships with peers. When children with autism trust their caregivers and educators, they are more likely to feel secure and confident in social settings. This confidence encourages social participation and interaction, leading to the development of meaningful friendships and connections with others. Trusting relationships also provide a safe space for practicing social skills and navigating social nuances, which

are fundamental for building and maintaining relationships.

5. Enhancing Learning Opportunities: Trust enhances learning opportunities for children with autism. When children trust their caregivers and educators, they are more receptive to instruction, guidance, and feedback. Trusting relationships create a positive learning environment where children feel supported, motivated, and empowered to explore new concepts and skills. This trust also encourages risk-taking and experimentation, fostering a growth mindset and a love for learning.

6. Strengthening Self-Esteem and Confidence: Building trust with children with autism boosts their self-esteem and confidence. When children feel valued, respected, and supported by their caregivers and educators, they develop a sense of self-worth and belief in their abilities. Trusting relationships provide opportunities for children to take on challenges, make mistakes, and learn from experiences, leading to increased self-confidence and resilience.

Building trust is essential for creating supportive, nurturing, and inclusive environments where they can thrive. Trusting relationships form the basis for effective communication, emotional regulation, social connection, learning, and self-esteem. By prioritizing trust-building strategies, caregivers and educators can lay the groundwork for the child's success and well-being, empowering them to reach their full potential.

NOTES

Understanding

Understanding a child with autism is like unearthing a treasure trove brimming with precious gems, a journey demanding patience, empathy, and abundant love. Just as each gem holds its own brilliance, every child with autism possesses unique qualities, quirks, and needs.

Understanding involves immersing oneself in their world, one that may appear unfamiliar, and viewing it through their perspective. It resembles embarking on an adventure together, where every day unveils fresh discoveries and insights. To truly understand a child necessitates dedicating time to listen, observe, and genuinely acquaint oneself with them.

Autism presents itself as a puzzle, with parents and teachers serving as the puzzle solvers. It involves identifying the pieces that seamlessly fit together to form a beautiful mosaic. Rather than seeking to alter the child, it entails embracing their individuality and fostering an environment where they can shine.

One of the most invaluable gifts bestowed upon a child with autism is acceptance. Embracing them in their entirety, quirks and all, signifies a profound expression of love. It requires relinquishing preconceived notions and relinquishing expectations, allowing the child to thrive authentically.

Understanding a child with autism also constitutes being a staunch advocate for their needs and facilitating their growth. It requires assuming the role of their voice when they are unable to articulate their needs, enabling them to receive the support and resources essential for their development.

Though the journey may pose its share of challenges, it is rich with moments of joy, laughter, and personal growth. By navigating these challenges, the child imparts invaluable lessons in patience, resilience, and the transformative power of love. Together, parents and teachers forge a bond with their child that transcends any obstacle encountered along the way.

Understimulation

Understimulation in children with autism can manifest in various ways. It occurs when a child's environment or activities do not provide enough sensory input or engagement to meet their needs. One common sign is a lack of interest and enthusiasm in their surroundings or interactions. Children who are understimulated may appear lethargic and disengaged. They may not show curiosity or excitement about the world around them. Another indicator can be repetitive behaviors. When children with autism are understimulated, they may engage in repetitive actions, such as hand-flapping or rocking, as a way to self-soothe or generate sensory input. These behaviors serve as a coping mechanism to compensate for the sensory deficit they are experiencing[120].

Withdrawal from social interactions is also a common response to understimulation. Children may prefer solitude or isolation because social interactions lack the sensory engagement they need. They might not respond to social cues or invitations to engage with others, making it challenging for them to connect with peers or family members. Restlessness can be another paradoxical sign of understimulation. Some children may become fidgety or hyperactive when they are not receiving enough sensory input. They might seek out sensory experiences or engage in stimming behaviors, such as finger-snapping or repetitive vocal sounds, to fulfill their sensory needs. Additionally, understimulation can affect a child's ability to focus and pay attention. They may struggle to maintain concentration during tasks or learning activities because their sensory needs are not being met, leading to distractibility and difficulty in completing activities[121].

In efforts to support a child who is experiencing understimulation, parents and teachers can take proactive steps. First, create an environment that offers a variety of sensory experiences, including tactile, visual, and auditory stimulation. Establish a structured daily routine that includes a balance of sensory-rich activities and opportunities for relaxation. Offering choices within the limits of sensory preferences can empower them to make decisions and feel more in control. Spending quality time engaging in activities of interest, such as reading a favorite book or going for a nature walk, can also provide valuable sensory input and strengthen your connection.

NOTES

Verbal Behavior

Verbal behavior, a concept introduced by behaviorist B.F. Skinner in 1957[122], is a theory that revolutionized our understanding of language acquisition and communication. It proposes that language is a learned behavior, shaped by environmental influences and subject to the principles of behaviorism. This means that language skills, including speaking, listening, and understanding, are acquired through interactions with our surroundings. Verbal behavior is crucial for children's language development and social interactions. It forms the foundation for communication, enabling individuals to express their needs, desires, thoughts, and emotions effectively. Understanding verbal behavior helps parents and teachers support children's language development and foster communication skills necessary for success in school and beyond. We often use verbal behavior without even realizing it in our everyday interactions. When we ask for something we want, label objects or actions, answer questions, repeat words or phrases, or follow directions, we are engaging in various components of verbal behavior. These behaviors are integral to effective communication and are present in countless situations throughout the day[123].

Understanding these components is essential for parents and teachers alike, as they form the building blocks of effective communication skills in children. Let's take a look at some components of verbal behavior:

1. Mand: Mands are requests or expressions of desires. A child saying, "Can I have a cookie, please?" is manding for a cookie. Parents can encourage manding by teaching their child to request what they want, promoting communication, self-advocacy, and independence.

2. Echoic: Echoic behavior involves repeating words or sounds heard from others. When a parent says, "Say 'apple,'" and the child repeats it, that's an echoic response. Parents can use echoic training to help their child develop clear and accurate pronunciation.

3. Motor Imitation: Motor imitation involves replicating physical actions observed in others. For example, when a child watches their teacher clap their hands and then imitates the action by clapping their own hands, they are demonstrating motor imitation. Teachers can promote motor imitation skills by providing clear demonstrations of actions and encouraging students to mimic those actions, thereby enhancing their ability to learn and perform motor tasks effectively.

4. Listener Responding: Listener responding involves understanding and responding to others' statements or questions, such as following directions. When a child complies with a direction like "Give me the ball," it's a listener response. Parents can reinforce listener responding by giving clear directions during daily routines and offering praise when their child complies.

5. Tact: Tacting involves labeling or describing objects, actions, or events in the environment. For instance, pointing at a dog and saying "Dog!" is a tacting response. Parents can support tacting by consistently labeling objects and actions during daily activities, thus enriching their child's vocabulary.

6. Intraverbal: Intraverbals are responses to questions or engaging in conversation. Answering questions like "What color is the sky?" with "Blue" is an intraverbal. Parents can foster intraverbal skills by engaging in

meaningful conversations with their child, encouraging expressive language.

Understanding and incorporating the components of verbal behavior into daily interactions can significantly enhance language development and communication skills in children. By recognizing the importance of manding, tacting, intraverbal behavior, echoic responses, and listener responding, parents and teachers can create supportive environments that foster language acquisition and social interactions. Through consistent practice, encouragement, and reinforcement, children can strengthen their verbal abilities, express themselves more effectively, and engage more confidently with the world around them. With these foundational skills in place, children are better equipped to navigate academic, social, and everyday situations, laying the groundwork for success in the future.

Visuals

Using visuals, including tools like the Picture Exchange Communication System (PECS), holds tremendous significance in supporting children with autism, benefiting both parents and teachers alike. Visual supports play a pivotal role in addressing the communication and behavioral challenges that many children on the autism spectrum face. Visuals provide a lifeline for enhanced communication, serving as an alternative means for children with autism to convey their needs, feelings, and desires. By utilizing pictures or symbols, these children can bridge the communication gap, reducing frustration and empowering them to communicate more effectively with their caregivers and peers[124]. Beyond communication, visuals significantly contribute to improved understanding. Many children with autism excel in visual thinking, and visual supports offer a concrete and tangible way to convey information. Visuals help these children better comprehend instructions, routines, and abstract concepts, leading to improved compliance and cooperation in daily activities.

Furthermore, visuals offer a sense of predictability and routine. Visual schedules and routines provide a clear roadmap of what to expect throughout the day, reducing anxiety and mitigating resistance to change for children with autism. Additionally, visual reinforcement is a powerful aspect of visual supports that parents and teachers can leverage. Establishing clear connections between behaviors and consequences using visual charts or systems can be highly motivating for children with autism, encouraging them to engage in positive behaviors consistently[125].

Parents and teachers can create a PECS binder filled with pictures of common items or actions that children might want to request, offering a customizable and accessible communication tool. Visual schedules and routines can be created using pictures or symbols to outline daily activities, providing structure and predictability for children with autism. Social stories with pictures can be developed to explain social situations, emotions, or expected behaviors, guiding children through various scenarios]. Incorporating "First-Then" boards with pictures can motivate children to complete tasks by visually showing the sequence of activities. Additionally, visual reinforcement charts can track and reward desired behaviors, promoting positive reinforcement and motivation.

Consistency and patience are key when implementing visual supports, requiring collaborative efforts between parents and teachers. While children may initially require guidance in using visuals, with time and practice, they can become more independent in utilizing these tools for communication and understanding, ultimately enhancing their overall development and well-being.

Vocational Skills

Vocational skills, often referred to as job or career skills, are fundamental abilities and knowledge that individuals need to perform tasks and responsibilities effectively in various work settings. While the development of these skills typically intensifies as children approach adolescence, the groundwork for acquiring vocational skills can be laid much earlier during childhood.

Examples of vocational skills encompass a wide range of abilities, such as communication skills, social skills, time management, problem-solving, computer literacy, work ethic, and task-specific skills relevant to one's interests and career aspirations. These skills collectively prepare individuals to navigate the demands of the workplace, contribute to society, and achieve independence.

Parents play a crucial role in helping their children learn and develop these vital vocational skills. Early exposure to the concept of work and different job roles can be beneficial. Visiting workplaces, discussing various careers, and sharing personal job experiences can pique a child's interest and provide context.

Teaching essential life skills is an excellent starting point. Skills like hygiene, organization, and self-care provide a foundation for more complex vocational abilities. Parents can introduce structured tasks and responsibilities at home, emphasizing the importance of completing them on time and to the best of their ability. These early experiences instill a sense of responsibility and time management.

Effective communication is another skill that can be nurtured from an early age. Encouraging children to engage in conversations, ask questions, and express themselves helps build their communication abilities. Modeling active listening and providing opportunities for children to practice these skills is essential.

Socialization is a significant aspect of vocational development. Facilitating interactions with peers through playdates, group activities, or social skills groups allows children to develop the social competence necessary for the workplace. These interactions teach collaboration, empathy, and teamwork.

As children approach adolescence, transition planning becomes important. Collaborating with teachers and specialists to create a transition plan that includes vocational goals can guide the development of specific skills and job-related experiences. Internships, job shadowing, or volunteer work in areas of interest provide real-world experiences that enhance vocational skills and provide insights into potential career paths.

Teachers are instrumental in facilitating their students' acquisition of vocational skills and a vital aspect of preparing them for future success in the workforce. They can achieve this through various means, beginning with the integration of vocational education programs into the school curriculum. These programs offer hands-on learning experiences across a spectrum of vocational fields, including carpentry, automotive repair, culinary arts, and computer technology, providing students with practical skills and exposing them to potential career paths[126].

Additionally, teachers can organize career exploration activities such as guest speakers, field trips, and career fairs, enabling students to identify their interests, strengths, and career goals. Job shadowing and internships arranged by teachers allow students to gain firsthand experience in professional environments, observe job responsibilities, and develop crucial workplace skills like communication and problem-solving. Teachers also incorporate life skills training into the curriculum, covering topics such as resume writing, job search strategies, and workplace etiquette to equip students with the essential skills for independent living and employment. Individualized support is provided to students with diverse learning needs, ensuring that all students have access to vocational education and training opportunities tailored to their specific requirements.

Collaboration with community partners, including employers and vocational rehabilitation agencies, expands vocational education opportunities for students and enriches their learning experience with valuable resources and mentorship opportunities. By emphasizing the development of soft skills such as communication, teamwork, and adaptability, teachers prepare students to become well-rounded and employable individuals, ready to thrive in the dynamic world of work. Through these strategies, teachers empower their students to explore career pathways, acquire essential vocational skills, and achieve their full potential in the workforce[127].

Advocating for support from schools and organizations is vital. By focusing on communication, socialization, time management, and specific job-related abilities, parents can empower their children with autism to thrive in the workforce and achieve greater independence in their lives. The journey of acquiring vocational skills is a gradual process, but with patience and dedication, children with autism can build a solid foundation for a successful and fulfilling future.

NOTES

Watch your mouth

This can't be stressed enough: Just because a child may not be able to speak does not mean that they can't hear you! Have you ever considered how you might feel if you constantly heard people talking about you, your deficits, your flaws, things you have no control over right in front of you as if you weren't there? Or how you might behave if the things you heard being said about you were actually untrue and you had no way to defend yourself. Speaking negatively about a child with autism in front of them, like speaking negatively about any child, can have profound and lasting effects. Many children with autism are highly perceptive and sensitive to the opinions and comments of adults, particularly parents and caregivers. Negative comments can severely impact their self-esteem and self-worth. For a child with autism, who may already face challenges in social and communication skills, negative talk can reinforce feelings of isolation and difference, potentially exacerbating those challenges.

Children learn by observing and mimicking the behavior of those around them. When adults engage in negative talk, they model a pattern of communication that the child may then replicate. This can lead to the development of negative self-talk in the child, where they internalize and repeat these harmful messages about themselves. Additionally, many individuals with autism have a literal understanding of language. Negative comments might be interpreted very directly, leading to confusion, hurt, or a skewed perception of self. The subtleties of sarcasm or exaggeration, often present in negative speech, may not be fully grasped, and the child might believe these negative comments are true and unexaggerated reflections of themselves.

Speaking negatively about a child can erode the trust in the parent-child or teacher-student relationship. Trust is foundational in any relationship, but for children with autism, who may struggle with understanding social cues and relationships, it is even more crucial. A breach in this trust can make it harder for them to feel safe and supported, which is essential for their development and learning. Hearing negative comments about themselves can lead to behavioral issues as well. They might act out as a form of expressing their distress or withdraw and become more isolated, which can hinder their social and emotional development.

It's also helpful to include them in conversations that are about them. No one likes to be talked about as if they are not present. Try including them in the conversation by talking to them, saying a quick phrase that acknowledges their presence, or reference something that they can connect with in the conversation. Let me give you some examples:

Including by talking to them:
• Instead of saying: "Albert had a bad day today." when speaking to someone else.
• Try: Turning to Albert and saying, "Albert, you had a bad day today but that's ok. We are going to try again tomorrow."
Saying a quick phrase to acknowledge their presence:
• Instead of saying: "Kenny doesn't like carrots." when talking to someone else.
• Say: "Kenny doesn't like carrots." Then turn to Kenny and say, "Don't worry, I won't make you eat the carrots."
Referencing something they can connect to:
• Instead of saying: "Lilly hates loud noises. Every time she hears a loud noise she cries."

• Try: "Lilly hates loud noises." Turn to Lilly and say, "Remember when the fire alarm went off and you were so sad because it hurt your ears."

There's a phrase in the autism community: "Nothing about us, without us." This simply means that decisions should not be made about persons with autism without the input of persons with autism. Try to apply this to your daily conversations about your child. This may take practice but this it's a worthy investment in nurturing your relationship with your child or student. You'll also notice the more you do it, the more others around you change their behavior as well.

Will

Parents, this one is just for you! One of the most significant steps you can take to secure your child's future is creating a Last Will and Testament. This document, often overshadowed by the day-to-day demands of parenting, is a fundamental pillar in safeguarding that your child is cared for according to your wishes, especially in scenarios that are difficult to think about but important to plan for[128].

A Last Will and Testament allows you to appoint a guardian for your child, someone who you trust and who understands the needs and gifts of your child. This decision is particularly crucial for a child with autism, as their needs might be specific and require a guardian equipped with knowledge, patience, and empathy. Additionally, your will can outline financial arrangements, like a special needs trust, to protect your child's financial future so that it remains secure and is managed in a way that benefits them, without jeopardizing any government benefits they may be entitled to.

Now, let's talk about how to get this important document in place. The process might seem daunting, but it's more approachable than you think. The first step is to consider consulting with an attorney who specializes in estate planning and has experience with special needs. This expertise is vital to navigate the complexities of your situation. The attorney can guide you through the process of drafting a will, setting up trusts, and verifying that all legal aspects are correctly handled. If the cost of an attorney seems prohibitive, look for legal aid societies or non-profit organizations that might offer discounted or pro bono services for families with special needs[129].

Additionally, it's advisable to involve your family and any potential guardians in these conversations. Open, heartfelt discussions about your wishes and the needs of your child can establish that everyone is on the same page and willing to take on the roles you're envisioning for them. Remember, the process of creating a Last Will and Testament is not just a legal task; it's an act of love and care, a way to provide for and protect your child, even when you're not physically present. While it can be emotionally challenging to consider these matters, taking the step to create a Last Will and Testament is a profound expression of love and responsibility. It's a way to be proactive so that your child's future is shaped by your deep understanding of their needs and your hopes for their well-being, regardless of what the future holds[130].

Weighted Blankets/Vests

Weighted blankets and vests are indeed invaluable tools for children with autism, have sensory properties that offer a myriad of benefits. Their effectiveness lies in their ability to provide deep pressure touch stimulation (DPTS), which can profoundly impact various aspects of a child's well-being. Many children with autism experience sensory processing issues, where they may be hypersensitive or hyposensitive to sensory stimuli. Weighted blankets offer a cocoon-like embrace, providing consistent, gentle pressure that can help integrate sensory information more effectively. This pressure aids in processing sensory stimuli in a more balanced manner, promoting a sense of calm and stability[131].

The pressure from a weighted blanket mimics the sensation of a firm hug, eliciting a calming effect similar to the release of serotonin, a neurotransmitter associated with relaxation. For children with autism who often grapple with heightened levels of anxiety, this effect can be particularly transformative. By reducing anxiety and fostering a sense of security, weighted blankets contribute to improved emotional regulation and overall well-being. Sleep disturbances are another common challenge. The soothing effect of weighted blankets helps calm the nervous system, making it easier for them to fall asleep and stay asleep throughout the night. Better sleep not only enhances mood and functioning but is also vital for their development and daily performance.

In educational settings, weighted blankets, stuffed animals or vests can aid in improving focus and attention. By providing a grounding effect, they help mitigate the impact of external stimuli, enabling children to better engage in classroom activities and tasks that require sustained concentration.

Weighted items can serve as invaluable tools during transitions, which can be particularly daunting for some children. Offering a consistent source of comfort and security, they facilitate a smoother transition between activities or environments, reducing stress and facilitating adaptive coping mechanisms. The calming effect of weighted items can contribute to a reduction in meltdowns and self-stimulatory behaviors (stimming). By mitigating sensory overload and providing a regulated sensory environment, they help alleviate the triggers that often precipitate meltdowns. The sensory input provided by the garment or object can lessen the need for certain self-stimulatory behaviors, promoting greater self-regulation[132].

While weighted items offer numerous benefits, it's important to acknowledge that they may not be suitable for everyone, and preferences can vary significantly among individuals with autism. Consulting with an occupational therapist or healthcare professional experienced in autism and sensory processing issues is essential to determine the appropriateness of a weighted blanket and facilitate its effective use. For example, using too much or too little weight can greatly alter effectiveness and comfort. It is typically recommended to not exceed one to two pounds over 10% of the person's body weight.

WTF

"A" may indeed stand for autism, but "W" could certainly stand for "What the *?#!" (insert favorite explicative). Acknowledging that children can prompt a scream of WT*?#! from the adults in their lives, whether once, twice, or perhaps one thousand seven hundred thirty eight times, is not just realistic—it's practically a requirement. Whether as a parent or a teacher, encountering those bewildering moments when nothing seems to make sense is a part of the journey with autism.

It's completely acceptable to find oneself in situations that are baffling and overwhelming. It's a shared experience among those who guide and nurture children with autism.

After all, does one truly understand the depth of autism without these hair-pulling moments? These aren't just challenges; they're markers of a path less traveled, where each step forward is a victory.

So, to all the dedicated parents and teachers out there, wear those WT* badges with honor. Let out a hearty laugh in the face of the pandemonium, and keep in mind that the role being played is not just about guiding a child through life but nurturing a remarkable individual who perceives the world in an extraordinary way. This journey is filled with trials and triumphs. Keep championing this cause, for the impact made on these wonderful children is both profound and lasting. Know that you're doing a spectacular job even if they can't tell you.

NOTES

XOXO (Hugs and Kisses)

Each child with autism may have their distinct reaction to physical affection. While some may welcome hugs and kisses with open arms, others may find them overwhelming or uncomfortable. A crucial aspect to consider is sensory sensitivities. Autism often comes with heightened sensory experiences, where hugs and kisses can feel too intense for some children. It can feel like being trapped in a tight squeeze or having your personal space invaded. It's vital for us to recognize these sensitivities and respect their boundaries, as pushing physical affection can lead to increased anxiety and stress for the child.

Respecting boundaries is paramount, much like with any child. We must honor the preferences of children with autism when it comes to affection. If they're not comfortable with hugs and kisses, forcing these actions can have adverse effects. Instead, we need to explore alternative ways to express our love and care, aligning with their comfort levels and needs.

Now, let's explore some creative avenues for showing affection beyond physical touch:

1. Quality time is another avenue to explore. Engage in activities that resonate with their interests. Whether it's playing their favorite game, reading together, or simply being present, this dedicated time speaks volumes.

2. Acts of kindness can be incredibly meaningful. Prepare their favorite meal, leave surprise notes, or offer assistance with tasks they find challenging. These gestures demonstrate your love and care in tangible ways.

3. Shared interests can strengthen bonds. Discover what they're passionate about and explore those interests together. Whether it's a hobby or topic they adore, dive into it alongside them, fostering connection and understanding.

4. Observation and communication play pivotal roles. Pay attention to their cues and preferences, and communicate openly about affection. If they respond positively to certain gestures like a high-five or a pat on the back, embrace those expressions of comfort.

5. Incorporating visual aids like social stories can also be beneficial. These tools help children understand and express their feelings about physical affection, fostering communication and mutual understanding.

6. Verbal affirmations are a dynamic way to convey love. Use words to express how much you love them, appreciate them, and are proud of them. Your words hold the warmth of your feelings, even without physical contact.

NOTES

Youth Programs

Incorporating children with autism into youth programs and recreational activities, such as sports and other hobbies, is a wonderful way to enrich their lives and promote inclusive environments. The significance lies in thoughtful adaptation and awareness, ensuring these experiences are positive and beneficial for all involved.

Start by recognizing the strengths and challenges each child with autism brings. Some children may excel in structured, rule-based activities like martial arts or swimming, where they can engage at their own pace and in a predictable environment. Others might find joy and success in creative endeavors like art classes or music lessons, where expression is more freeform and less bound by strict rules or physical exertion. The choice of activity should align with the child's interests and sensory preferences, creating an inviting and comfortable space for them to explore and grow[130].

Adaptation of these programs is often necessary. Instructors and program leaders should be knowledgeable about autism and prepared to make reasonable accommodations. This could mean smaller class sizes, a quieter environment, or a more flexible approach to instruction, allowing children with autism to participate without feeling overwhelmed or out of place. It's also beneficial to have a consistent routine within the activity.

Be sure to communicate your child's specific needs, triggers, and effective strategies to the coaches or instructors for engagement and support. This collaboration ensures that the program is tailored to the child's individual requirements, enhancing their ability to participate and enjoy the activity. It's also important to foster an environment of inclusion and understanding among all participants. Educating peers about autism and promoting an atmosphere of acceptance and kindness goes a long way in making these programs successful for children with autism. This not only benefits the children with autism but also teaches other participants empathy, diversity, and the value of inclusivity.

Lastly, celebrating successes, no matter how small, is pivotal. Whether it's mastering a new skill, participating in a team effort, or simply enjoying the activity, these achievements should be acknowledged and celebrated. This encouragement reinforces positive experiences and builds self-esteem in children with autism, encouraging them to continue engaging in such activities[134].

Involvement in youth programs and recreational activities can be incredibly rewarding, offering opportunities to develop new skills, make social connections, and experience the joys of play and creativity in a supportive environment. It's about creating spaces where they can thrive, feel valued, and be part of a community.

NOTES

Zero Tolerance

Creating a nurturing and supportive environment for a child with autism is essential, both at home and in school settings. Parents and teachers must collaboratively foster a space where all children, particularly those with autism, feel not just included, but genuinely valued and supported.

This supportive environment is critical in helping children thrive by recognizing their challenges and strengths, and providing the tailored support they need for optimal development and well-being. To achieve this, it's crucial that both parents and educators adopt a zero-tolerance stance towards any behaviors, attitudes, or practices that could undermine the growth and dignity of children with autism.

This involves proactive engagement, vigilant oversight, and consistent action to ensure that their environment is not only safe but also enriching. This commitment requires a clear understanding and enforcement of certain non-negotiable standards, which include advocating for the child's needs, challenging harmful stereotypes, and ensuring access to appropriate educational and developmental resources.

By holding these standards, parents and teachers can truly make a significant difference in the lives of children with autism, helping them to achieve their full potential and feel truly integrated within their communities and peer groups. Here is a list of areas where zero tolerance can be enforced to cultivate such an environment.

1. Bullying and Discrimination: Immediate action must be taken against any form of bullying or discrimination,

whether it occurs in school, within the community, or online.

2. Misinformation about Autism: Both parents and teachers should reject pseudoscience and unproven 'cures' or treatments, focusing instead on evidence based, scientifically-supported practices and information.

3. Lowered Expectations: It's crucial to maintain high expectations. Underestimating a child's abilities due to their autism does a great disservice. As Les Brown famously said, "No one rises to low expectations."

4. Inadequate Educational Support: Ensuring that each child receives the necessary educational accommodations and support to succeed is absolutely fundamental.

5. Social Exclusion: Advocacy for inclusion in social activities and a firm stance against social isolation are key for fostering proper social development.

6. Negative Speech or Attitudes: Negative talk about autism, whether at home, in school, or in the media, is unacceptable. A positive and understanding perspective of autism should be promoted at all times.

7. Inflexibility in Routines and Approaches: The need for adaptable strategies and routines to cater to a child's needs must be recognized and implemented.

8. Lack of Professional Support When Needed: Both parents and educators should ensure that they seek and accept help from qualified professionals to support the child's development effectively.

9. Ignoring the Child's Voice and Perspective: Children with autism express their own views and feelings, which should always be acknowledged and respected.

10. Overlooking Self-Care: The airplane oxygen mask analogy is apt—take care of your own mental and physical health to be able to fully support the child.

11. Ignoring Sensory Sensitivities: Sensitivities such as those to light, sound, or textures must be taken seriously to avoid causing distress to the child.

12. Forcing Social Interaction: Forcing children into social settings without proper support can be counterproductive and stressful.

13. Disrespecting Personal Boundaries: Respecting personal boundaries is crucial for building trust and security, especially for children with autism.

14. Inflexible Communication Methods: Adapting communication styles to fit the child's needs, such as using visual aids or simplifying language, is critical for effective interaction.

15. Ignoring Behavioral Cues: All behavior is a form of communication. These cues should not be overlooked as they are critical for understanding and connecting with the child.

16. Unqualified or Inappropriate Therapy: Only therapies and therapists specialized in and experienced with autism should be utilized to prevent potential harm.

17. Stigmatizing Language or Attitudes in Their Environment: Any stigmatizing language or attitudes,

whether in school, at home, or in the broader community, must be actively challenged and corrected.

18. Ignoring the Need for Routine: Routines are incredibly important and should not be disrupted without necessary preparation.

19. Overlooking Nutrition and Physical Health: Balanced nutrition and appropriate physical activity are essential for all children, including those with autism.

20. Lack of Individualized Education Plan (IEP) Involvement: Parents and teachers must be actively involved in the creation and ongoing adaptation of the child's IEP to ensure it meets their evolving needs.

21. Neglecting Social Skills Development: Opportunities for developing social skills should be provided in a supportive setting, respecting the child's comfort level.

22. Ignoring the Child's Interests: Engaging with and encouraging a child's specific, intense interests can be a powerful educational tool.

23. Failure to Celebrate Achievements: Recognizing and celebrating achievements, no matter how small, is vital for building self-esteem and motivation.

24. Lack of Collaboration with Caregivers and Professionals: Effective support often requires teamwork among parents, teachers, therapists, and other caregivers.

25. Not Preparing for Transitions: Both daily and life-stage transitions require careful preparation and support to ensure they are managed smoothly.

Adhering to these principles helps create an environment where children with autism can thrive both academically and personally.

Glossary

References

[1] American Psychiatric Association. (2013). Diagnostic and statistical manual of mental disorders (5th ed.). Arlington, VA: American Psychiatric Publishing

[2] Centers for Disease Control and Prevention. (2020). Autism spectrum disorder (ASD). Retrieved from https://www.cdc.gov

[3] Beukelman, D. R., & Mirenda, P. (2013). Augmentative and alternative communication: Supporting children and adults with complex communication needs (4th ed.). Baltimore, MD: Paul H. Brookes Publishing Co.

[4] American Speech-Language-Hearing Association. (2021). Augmentative and alternative communication (AAC). Retrieved from https://www.asha.org/public/speech/disorders/AAC/

[5] Light, J. C., & McNaughton, D. (2015). Communicative competence for individuals who require augmentative and alternative communication: A new definition for a new era of communication? Augmentative and Alternative Communication, 31(1), 1-18. https://doi.org/10.3109/07434618.2014.1001793

[6] Cooper, J. O., Heron, T. E., & Heward, W. L. (2020). Applied behavior analysis (3rd ed.). New York, NY: Pearson

[7] Leaf, J. B., McEachin, J., Taubman, M., & Leaf, R. (2016). Controversial issues in the behavioral treatment of autism. New York, NY: Springer.

[8] U.S. Department of Justice. (n.d.). Americans with Disabilities Act (ADA). https://www.ada.gov/law-and-regs/ada/

[9] Matson, J. L., Hattier, M. A., & Belva, B. (2012). Treating adaptive living skills of persons with autism using applied behavior analysis: A review. Research in Autism Spectrum Disorders, 6(1), 271-276. https://doi.org/10.1016/j.rasd.2011.05.008

[10] Odom, S. L., Collet-Klingenberg, L., Rogers, S. J., & Hatton, D. D. (2010). Evidence-based practices in interventions for children and youth with autism spectrum disorders. Preventing School Failure: Alternative Education for Children and Youth, 54(4), 275-282. https://doi.org/10.1080/10459881003785506

[11] Lovaas, O. I. (1987). Behavioral treatment and normal educational and intellectual functioning in young autistic children. Journal of Consulting and Clinical Psychology, 55(1), 3-9. https://doi.org/10.1037/0022-006X.55.1.3

[12] Shattuck, P. T., Wagner, M., Narendorf, S., Sterzing, P., & Hensley, M. (2012). Post-high school service use among young adults with an autism

spectrum disorder. Archives of Pediatrics & Adolescent Medicine, 166(2), 183-189. https://doi.org/10.1001/archpediatrics.2011.390

[13] Migliore, A., Timmons, J. C., Butterworth, J., & Lugas, J. (2012). Predictors of employment and postsecondary education of youth with autism. Rehabilitation Counseling Bulletin, 55(3), 176-184. https://doi.org/10.1177/0034355212438943

[14] National Center for Learning Disabilities. (2017). IDEA Parent Guide. https://www.advocacyinstitute.org/resources/IDEA2004parentguide.pdf

[15] Behavior Analyst Certification Board. (2023). BCBA certification. Retrieved from https://www.bacb.com/bcba/

[16] Hanley, M. H., Iwata, B. A., & Ingersoll, T. E. (2009). Behavioral interventions for self-injurious behavior. Behavior Analyst Today, 10(1), 3-9.

[17] Behavior Analyst Certification Board. (2023). Behavior intervention plan. Retrieved from https://www.bacb.com/behavior-intervention-plan/

[18] Attwood, T. (2007). The complete guide to Asperger's syndrome. London, UK: Jessica Kingsley Publishers.

[19] Grandin, T. (1995). Thinking in pictures: And other reports from my life with autism. New York, NY: Vintage Books.

[20] Bal, V. H., Katz, T., Bishop, S. L., & Krasileva, K. (2016). Understanding definitions of minimally verbal across instruments: evidence for subgroups within minimally verbal children and adolescents with autism spectrum disorder. Journal of child psychology and psychiatry, and allied disciplines, 57(12), 1424–1433.

[21] Paul, R., & Norbury, C. F. (2012). Language disorders from infancy through adolescence: Listening, speaking, reading, writing, and communicating (4th ed.). St. Louis, MO: Elsevier.

[22] Elsabbagh, M., Divan, G., Koh, Y. J., Kim, Y. S., Kauchali, S., Marcín, C., ... & Bahl, J. M. (2012). Global prevalence of autism and other pervasive developmental disorders. Autism research, 15(1), 160-179. https://onlinelibrary.wiley.com/doi/epdf/10.1002/aur.239

[23] Sugai, G., & Horner, R. H. (2009). Peer-mediated interventions for enhancing school behavior: A review of the literature. School Psychology Quarterly, 24(1), 33-51. https://dropoutprevention.org/wp-content/uploads/2015/07/Sugai__Horner_2009_exceptionality_RTI__SWPBS_Integration_SolutionsFeb2011.pdf

[24] Howlin, P. (2013). Social disadvantage and exclusion: Adults with autism lag far behind in the race for social inclusion. Journal of Autism and

Developmental Disorders, 43, 1602-1607. https://doi.org/10.1007/
s10803-012-1710-8

[25] National Autistic Society. (2021). Choosing the right day service for an
autistic person. Retrieved from https://www.autism.org.uk

[26] Centers for Disease Control and Prevention. (2023, June 5). Act Early: If
You're Concerned About Your Child's Development. https://www.cdc.gov/
ncbddd/actearly/index.html

[27] Mazurek, M. O., Vasa, R. A., Kalb, L. G., Kanne, S. M., Rosenberg, D.,
Keefer, A., ... & Lowery, L. A. (2013). Anxiety, sensory over-responsivity, and
gastrointestinal problems in children with autism spectrum disorders. Journal
of Abnormal Child Psychology, 41, 165-176. https://doi.org/10.1007/
s10802-012-9668-x

[28] Sathe, N., Andrews, J. C., McPheeters, M. L., & Warren, Z. (2017).
Nutritional and dietary interventions for autism spectrum disorder: A
systematic review. Pediatrics, 139(6), e20170346. https://doi.org/10.1542/
peds.2017-0346

[29] Lovaas, O. I. (1987). Behavioral treatment and normal educational and
intellectual functioning in young autistic children. Journal of Consulting and
Clinical Psychology, 55(1), 3-9. https://doi.org/10.1037/0022-006X.55.1.3

[30] Dziuk, G. A., Lane, A. E., & Balogh, M. (2007). Praxis in autism spectrum
disorders: A review of the literature. Developmental Neuropsychology, 32(2),
239-268.

[31] Larsson, B. (2012). The benefits of early intervention for children with
autism spectrum disorders. The OSSA Conference & Expo 2012.
[10] Ingersoll, J. M., Lai, M. T., Gotham, K., & Miller, J. L. (2013). Occurrence
and family impact of elopement in children with autism spectrum disorders.
Journal of Child Psychology and Psychiatry, 54(5), 870-877. https://
pubmed.ncbi.nlm.nih.gov/23045563/

[32] Stiegler, L. N. (2015). Examining the echolalia literature: Where do
speech-language pathologists stand? American Journal of Speech-Language
Pathology, 24(4), 750-762. https://doi.org/10.1044/2015_AJSLP-15-0016

[33] Karmiloff, K., & Karmiloff-Smith, A. (2002). Pathways to language: From
fetus to adolescent. Cambridge, MA: Harvard University Press.

[34] National Center for Learning Disabilities. (2021). Understanding IEPs and
504 plans. Retrieved from https://www.ncld.org

[35] Zirkel, P. A. (2017). The law of special education: Examples and
explanations (4th ed.). Frederick, MD: Aspen Publishers.

[36] Anderson, C., Law, J. K., Daniels, A., Rice, C., Mandell, D. S., Hagopian, L., & Law, P. A. (2012). Occurrence and family impact of elopement in children with autism spectrum disorders. Journal of Child Psychology and Psychiatry, 53(5), 487-495. https://doi.org/10.1111/j.1469-7610.2012.02508.x

[37] Samson, A. C., Huber, O., & Gross, J. J. (2015). Emotion regulation in Asperger's syndrome and high-functioning autism. Emotion, 12(4), 659-665. https://doi.org/10.1037/a0027975

[38] Gioia, G. A., Isquith, P. K., Guy, S. C., & Kenworthy, L. (2015). Behavior rating inventory of executive function. Lutz, FL: Psychological Assessment Resources

[39] Hill, E. L. (2004). Executive dysfunction in autism. Trends in Cognitive Sciences, 8(1), 26-32. https://doi.org/10.1016/j.tics.2003.11.003

[40] Dawson, P., & Guare, R. (2018). Smart but scattered: The revolutionary "executive skills" approach to helping kids reach their potential. New York, NY: Guilford Press.

[41] Owens, R. E. (2015). Language development: An introduction (9th ed.). Upper Saddle River, NJ: Pearson.

[42] Sussman, F. (2012). More than words: Helping parents promote communication and social skills in children with autism spectrum disorder. Toronto, ON: The Hanen Centre.

[43] Hodgdon, L. Q. (2012). Visual strategies for improving communication: Practical supports for school and home (2nd ed.). Troy, MI: QuirkRoberts Publishing.

[44] U.S. Department of Education. (2020, August 28). Section 504 and Students with Disabilities.

[45] Individuals with Disabilities Education Act, 20 U.S.C. § 1400 (2004). Retrieved from https://sites.ed.gov/idea

[46] Boyd, B. A., Conroy, M. A., Mancil, G. R., Nakao, T., & Alter, P. J. (2007). Effects of circumscribed interests on the social behaviors of children with autism spectrum disorders. Journal of Autism and Developmental Disorders, 37(8), 1550-1561. https://doi.org/10.1007/s10803-006-0286-8

[47] Buie, T., Campbell, D. B., Fuchs, G. J., Furuta, G. T., Levy, J., VandeWater, J., & Whitaker, A. H. (2010). Evaluation, diagnosis, and treatment of gastrointestinal disorders in individuals with ASDs: A consensus report. Pediatrics, 125(Supplement 1), S1-S18. https://doi.org/10.1542/peds.2009-1878C

[48] U.S. Department of Education. (2020, August 28). Section 504 and Students with Disabilities.

[49] McElhanon, B. O., McCracken, C., Karpen, S., & Sharp, W. G. (2014). Gastrointestinal symptoms in autism spectrum disorder: A meta-analysis. Pediatrics, 133(5), 872-883. https://doi.org/10.1542/peds.2013-3995

[50] Stokes, T. F., & Baer, D. M. (1977). An implicit technology of generalization. Journal of Applied Behavior Analysis, 10(2), 349-367. https://doi.org/10.1901/jaba.1977.10-349

[51] Baranek, G. T. (2002). Efficacy of sensory and motor interventions for children with autism. Journal of Autism and Developmental Disorders, 32(5), 397-422. https://doi.org/10.1023/A:1020541906063

[52] Baranek, G. T., David, F. J., Poe, M. D., Stone, W. L., & Watson, L. R. (2006). Sensory experiences questionnaire: Discriminating sensory features in young children with autism, developmental delays, and typical development. Journal of Child Psychology and Psychiatry, 47(6), 591-601. https://doi.org/10.1111/j.1469-7610.2005.01546.x

[53] Individuals with Disabilities Education Act. (2004). 20 U.S.C. § 1400 et seq.

[54] Yell, M. L., Katsiyannis, A., & Bradley, R. (2017). The Individuals with Disabilities Education Act: The evolution of special education law. In L. Florian (Ed.), The SAGE handbook of special education (2nd ed., pp. 103-124). Thousand Oaks, CA: SAGE Publications.

[55] Ingersoll, B. (2012). Brief report: Effect of a focused imitation intervention on social functioning in children with autism. Journal of Autism and Developmental Disorders, 42(8), 1768-1773. https://doi.org/10.1007/s10803-011-1423-6

[56] Booth, T., & Ainscow, M. (2011). The Index for Inclusion: Developing learning and participation in schools (3rd ed.). Bristol, UK: Centre for Studies on Inclusive Education.

[57] Odom, S. L., Buysse, V., & Soukakou, E. (2011). Inclusion for young children with disabilities: A quarter century of research perspectives. Journal of Early Intervention, 33(4), 344-356. https://doi.org/10.1177/1053815111430094

[58] Souders, M. C., Zavodny, S., Eriksen, W., Sinko, R., Connell, J., Kerns, C., Schaaf, R., & Pinto-Martin, J. (2017). Sleep in Children with Autism Spectrum Disorder. Current psychiatry reports, 19(6), 34. https://doi.org/10.1007/s11920-017-0782-x American Association on Intellectual and Developmental Disabilities (AAIDD). (2010). Intellectual disability: Definition, classification, and systems of supports (11th ed.). https://www.aaidd.org/intellectual-disability/definition

[59] American Association on Intellectual and Developmental Disabilities (AAIDD). (2010). Intellectual disability: Definition, classification, and systems of supports (11th ed.). https://www.aaidd.org/intellectual-disability/definition

[60] American Association on Intellectual and Developmental Disabilities (AAIDD). (2010). Intellectual disability: Definition, classification, and systems of supports (11th ed.). Retrieved from https://www.aaidd.org/intellectual-disability/definition

[61] Fournier, K. A., Hass, C. J., Naik, S. K., Lodha, N., & Cauraugh, J. H. (2010). Motor coordination in autism spectrum disorders: A synthesis and meta-analysis. Journal of Autism and Developmental Disorders, 40(10), 1227-1240. https://doi.org/10.1007/s10803-010-0981-3

[62] Lord, C., & Paul, R. (1997). Language and communication in autism. In D. J. Cohen & F. R. Volkmar (Eds.), Handbook of autism and pervasive developmental disorders (2nd ed., pp. 195-225). Hoboken, NJ: John Wiley & Sons.

[63] Cooper, P., Drummond, M. J., Hart, S., Lovey, J., & McLaughlin, C. (2009). Positive alternatives to exclusion. Abingdon, UK: Routledge.

[64] Elias, M. J. (2014). Social-emotional skills can boost Common Core implementation. Phi Delta Kappan, 95(8), 58-62. https://doi.org/10.1177/003172171409500814

[65] Happe, F. G. (1993). Communicative competence and theory of mind in autism: A test of relevance theory. Cognition, 48(2), 101-119. https://doi.org/10.1016/0010-0277(93)90026-R

[66] Cohen, M., & Frea, W. D. (2004). Autism and self-control: Effects of sensory experiences on self-stimulation. Focus on Autism and Other Developmental Disabilities, 19(3), 133-140. https://doi.org/10.1177/10883576040190030201

[67] Yell, M. L. (2016). The law and special education (4th ed.). Upper Saddle River, NJ: Pearson.

[68] Bhat, A. N., Landa, R. J., & Galloway, J. C. (2011). Current perspectives on motor functioning in infants, children, and adults with autism spectrum disorders. Physical Therapy, 91(7), 1116-1129. https://doi.org/10.2522/ptj.20100294

[69] Gold, C., Wigram, T., & Elefant, C. (2006). Music therapy for autistic spectrum disorder. Cochrane Database of Systematic Reviews, 2. https://doi.org/10.1002/14651858.CD004381.pub2

[70] Ghasemtabar, S. N., Hosseini, M., Fayyaz, I., Arab, S., Naghashian, H., & Poudineh, Z. (2015). Music therapy: An effective approach in improving social

skills of children with autism. Advanced Biomedical Research, 4(1), 157. https://doi.org/10.4103/2277-9175.161553

[71] Ventola, P., Lei, J., Paisley, C., Lebowitz, E., & Silverman, W. (2017). Parenting a Child with ASD: Comparison of Parenting Style Between ASD, Anxiety, and Typical Development. Journal of autism and developmental disorders, 47(9), 2873–2884. https://doi.org/10.1007/s10803-017-3210-5

[72] Armstrong, T. (2010). The power of neurodiversity: Unleashing the advantages of your differently wired brain. Cambridge, MA: Da Capo Press.

[73] Singer, J. (1999). 'Why can't you be normal for once in your life?' From a 'problem with no name' to the emergence of a new category of difference. In M. Corker & S. French (Eds.), Disability discourse (pp. 59-67). Buckingham, UK: Open University Press.

[74] National Institute on Deafness and Other Communication Disorders. (2018). Statistics on voice, speech, and language. Retrieved from https://www.nidcd.nih.gov/health/statistics/statistics-voice-speech-and-language

[75] Kagan, J. (1998). Biological bases of childhood shyness. Science, 240(4853), 167-171. https://doi.org/10.1126/science.240.4853.167

[76] American Occupational Therapy Association. (2020). Occupational therapy practice framework: Domain and process(4th ed.). Bethesda, MD: AOTA Press

[77] American Speech-Language-Hearing Association. (2021). Oral-motor-based speech disorders. Retrieved from https://www.asha.org/practice-portal/clinical-topics/oral-motor-based-speech-disorders/

[78] Green, S. A., Ben-Sasson, A., Soto, T. W., & Carter, A. S. (2016). Anxiety and sensory over-responsivity in toddlers with autism spectrum disorders: Bidirectional effects across time. Journal of Autism and Developmental Disorders, 42(6), 1117-1128. https://doi.org/10.1007/s10803-011-1361-3

[79] Bondy, A., & Frost, L. (2011). The Picture Exchange Communication System. Behavior Modification, 25(5), 725-744. https://doi.org/10.1177/0145445501255004

[80] Bateman, B. D., & Cline, J. (2019). Special education law and policy: From the schoolhouse to the courthouse. Washington, DC: Council for Exceptional Children.

[81] Kasper, G., & Rose, K. R. (2001). Pragmatics in language teaching. In K. R. Rose & G. Kasper (Eds.), Pragmatics in language teaching (pp. 1-9). New York, NY: Cambridge University Press.

[82] American Physical Therapy Association. (2021). The role of physical therapy in health and wellness. Retrieved from https://www.apta.org/patient-care/why-choose-pt/physical-therapy-roles

[83] Oliveras-Rentas, R. E., Kenworthy, L., Roberson, R. B., Martin, A., & Wallace, G. L. (2012). WISC-IV profile in high-functioning autism spectrum disorders: Implications for the identification of autism spectrum disorders. Journal of Autism and Developmental Disorders, 42(3), 400-410. https://doi.org/10.1007/s10803-011-1250-9

[84] American Psychological Association. (2017). Clinical practice guideline for the evaluation of psychological disorders. Washington, DC: APA.

[85] Tager-Flusberg, H., & Joseph, R. M. (2003). Identifying neurocognitive phenotypes in autism. Philosophical Transactions of the Royal Society B: Biological Sciences, 358(1430), 303-314. https://doi.org/10.1098/rstb.2002.1198

[86] Behavior Analyst Certification Board. (2020). Registered Behavior Technician (RBT) handbook. Littleton, CO: BACB. Retrieved from https://www.bacb.com/wp-content/uploads/2020/11/RBT-2nd-Edition-Task-List.pdf

[87] Miltenberger, R. G. (2016). Behavior modification: Principles and procedures (6th ed.). Boston, MA: Cengage Learning.

[88] Cowen, P. S., & Reed, D. A. (2002). Effects of respite care for children with developmental disabilities: Evaluation of an intervention for at risk families. Public Health Nursing, 19(4), 272-283. https://doi.org/10.1046/j.1525-1446.2002.19406.x

[89] American Psychiatric Association. (2013). Diagnostic and statistical manual of mental disorders (5th ed.). Arlington, VA: American Psychiatric Publishing.

[90] Bellini, S., Peters, J. K., Benner, L., & Hopf, A. (2007). A meta-analysis of school-based social skills interventions for children with autism spectrum disorders. Remedial and Special Education, 28(3), 153-162. https://doi.org/10.1177/07419325070280030401

[91] Schneider, N., Williams, K., & Hibbert, K. (2007). Predictors of challenging behaviour in pre-school children with autism spectrum disorders. International Journal of Disability, Development and Education, 54(2), 187-201. https://doi.org/10.1080/10349120701330160

[92] Connie Anderson, J. Kiely Law, Amy Daniels, Catherine Rice, David S. Mandell, Louis Hagopian, Paul A. Law; Occurrence and Family Impact of Elopement in Children With Autism Spectrum Disorders. Pediatrics November 2012; 130 (5): 870–877. 10.1542/peds.2012-0762

[93] Leekam, S. R., Prior, M. R., & Uljarevic, M. (2011). Restricted and repetitive behaviors in autism spectrum disorders: A review of research in the last decade. Psychological Bulletin, 137(4), 562-593. https://doi.org/10.1037/a0023341

[94] Quill, K. A. (2000). Do-watch-listen-say: Social and communication intervention for children with autism. Baltimore, MD: Brookes Publishing.

[95] Wong, C., Odom, S. L., Hume, K., Cox, A. W., Fettig, A., Kucharczyk, S., ... & Schultz, T. R. (2015). Evidence-based practices for children, youth, and young adults with autism spectrum disorder: A comprehensive review. Journal of Autism and Developmental Disorders, 45(7), 1951-1966. https://doi.org/10.1007/s10803-014-2351-z

[96] Lovaas, O. I. (2003). Teaching individuals with developmental delays: Basic intervention techniques. Austin, TX: Pro-Ed.

[97] Leaf, R. B., & McEachin, J. J. (1999). A work in progress: Behavior management strategies and a curriculum for intensive behavioral treatment of autism. New York, NY: DRL Books.

[98] Shore, S. M. (2003). Beyond the wall: Personal experiences with autism and Asperger syndrome. Autism Asperger Publishing Company.

[99] Baker, D. L. (2011). The politics of neurodiversity: Why public policy matters. Boulder, CO: Lynne Rienner Publishers.

[100] Turnbull, R., Turnbull, A., & Wehmeyer, M. L. (2020). Exceptional lives: Special education in today's schools (9th ed.). Boston, MA: Pearson.

[101] Friend, M., & Bursuck, W. D. (2019). Including students with special needs: A practical guide for classroom teachers(8th ed.). New York, NY: Pearson.

[102] Kauffman, J. M., & Badar, J. (2018). Enduring issues in special education: Personal perspectives. New York, NY: Routledge.

[103] Ayres, A. J. (2005). Sensory integration and the child. Los Angeles, CA: Western Psychological Services.

[104] Pfeiffer, B., Koenig, K., Kinnealey, M., Sheppard, M., & Henderson, L. (2011). Effectiveness of sensory integration interventions in children with autism spectrum disorders: A pilot study. American Journal of Occupational Therapy, 65(1), 76-85. https://doi.org/10.5014/ajot.2011.09205

[105] Dunn, W. (2001). The sensations of everyday life: Empirical, theoretical, and pragmatic considerations. American Journal of Occupational Therapy, 55(6), 608-620. https://doi.org/10.5014/ajot.55.6.608

[106] Ayres, A. J. (2005). Sensory integration and the child. Los Angeles, CA: Western Psychological Services.

[107] Parham, L. D., & Mailloux, Z. (2010). Sensory integration. In J. Case-Smith & J. C. O'Brien (Eds.), Occupational therapy for children (6th ed., pp. 325-372). St. Louis, MO: Mosby/Elsevier.

[108] Burrows, K. E., Adams, C. L., & Spiers, J. (2008). Sentinels of safety: Service dogs ensure safety and enhance freedom and well-being for families with autistic children. Qualitative Health Research, 18(12), 1642-1649. https://doi.org/10.1177/1049732308327088

[109] Berry, A., Borgi, M., Francia, N., Alleva, E., & Cirulli, F. (2013). Use of assistance and therapy dogs for children with autism spectrum disorders: A critical review of the current evidence. Journal of Alternative and Complementary Medicine, 19(2), 73-80. https://doi.org/10.1089/acm.2011.0835

[110] Howlin, P., Baron-Cohen, S., & Hadwin, J. (2009). Teaching children with autism to mind-read: A practical guide for teachers and parents. New York, NY: Wiley.

[111] Gray, C., Broek, E., Cain, S. L., Dutkiewicz, M., Fleck, C., Gray, B., Gray, J., Jonker, S., Lindrup, A., & Moore, L. (Eds.). (1993). The social story book

[112] Kuoch, H., & Mirenda, P. (2003). Social story interventions for young children with autism spectrum disorders. Focus on Autism and Other Developmental Disabilities, 18(4), 219-227. https://doi.org/10.1177/10883576030180040301

[113] Paul, R. (2008). Language disorders from infancy through adolescence: Assessment and intervention (3rd ed.). St. Louis, MO: Mosby.

[114] Satter, E. (2000). Child of mine: Feeding with love and good sense (2nd ed.). Boulder, CO: Bull Publishing.

[115] Turner, M. (1999). Repetitive behaviour in autism: A review of psychological research. Journal of Child Psychology and Psychiatry, 40(6), 839-849. https://doi.org/10.1111/1469-7610.00502

[116] Bodfish, J. W., Symons, F. J., Parker, D. E., & Lewis, M. H. (2000). Varieties of repetitive behavior in autism: Comparisons to mental retardation. Journal of Autism and Developmental Disorders, 30(3), 237-243. https://doi.org/10.1023/A:1005596502855

[117] Potegal, M., & Davidson, R. J. (2003). Temper tantrums in young children: 1. Behavioral composition. Journal of Developmental & Behavioral Pediatrics, 24(3), 140-147. https://doi.org/10.1097/00004703-200306000-00003

[118] Myles, B. S., Southwick, J., Brooks, J. K., & Holliday-Willey, L. (2004). Understanding and addressing the needs of children and youth with Asperger syndrome and autism. Kansas City, MO: AAPC Publishing.

[119] Test, D. W., Mazzotti, V. L., Mustian, A. L., Fowler, C. H., Kortering, L., & Kohler, P. (2009). Evidence-based secondary transition predictors for improving postschool outcomes for students with disabilities. Career Development for Exceptional Individuals, 32(3), 160-181. https://doi.org/10.1177/0885728809346960

[120] Schaaf, R. C., & Lane, S. J. (2015). Toward a best-practice protocol for assessment of sensory features in ASD. Journal of Autism and Developmental Disorders, 45(5), 1380-1395. https://doi.org/10.1007/s10803-014-2299-5

[121] Lane, S. J., Young, R. L., Baker, A. E. Z., & Angley, M. T. (2010). Sensory processing subtypes in autism: Association with adaptive behavior. Journal of Autism and Developmental Disorders, 40(1), 112-122. https://doi.org/10.1007/s10803-009-0840-2

[122] Skinner, B. F. (1957). Verbal behavior. Appleton-Century-Crofts.

[123] Greer, R. D., & Ross, D. E. (2008). Verbal behavior analysis: Inducing and expanding new verbal capabilities in children with language delays. Boston, MA: Pearson.

[124] Frost, L. A., & Bondy, A. S. (2002). The Picture Exchange Communication System training manual (2nd ed.). Newark, DE: Pyramid Educational Consultants.

[125] Odom, S. L., Hume, K., Boyd, B. A., & Stabel, L. (2010). Moving beyond the intensive behavior treatment versus eclectic dichotomy: Evidence-based and individualized programs for learners with ASD. Behavior Modification, 34(3), 242-262. https://doi.org/10.1177/0145445510370877

[126] Stern, D., Stone, J. R., Hopkins, C., McMillion, M., & Crain, R. (1998). Benefits and costs of school-to-work: The employers' perspective. Washington, DC: Office of Educational Research and Improvement.

[127] Rojewski, J. W. (1999). Career-related predictors of work-bound and college-bound status of adolescents in rural and non-rural areas. Journal of Research in Rural Education, 15(3), 141-156. http://jrre.psu.edu/wp-content/uploads/2016/02/15-3_6.pdf

[128] Wright, P. W. D., & Wright, P. D. (2010). Wrightslaw: From emotions to advocacy: The special education survival guide. Hartfield, VA: Harbor House Law Press.

[129] Special Needs Alliance. (2015). Guide to planning for a child with special needs. Special Needs Alliance. Retrieved from https://www.specialneedsalliance.org/guide-to-planning/

[130] Guardianship and Trusts. (2020). Setting up a special needs trust: Essential considerations. Special Needs Alliance. Retrieved from https://www.specialneedsalliance.org

[131] Zissermann, L. (1992). The effects of deep pressure on self-stimulating behaviors in a child with autism and other disabilities. American Journal of Occupational Therapy, 46(6), 547-551. https://doi.org/10.5014/ajot.46.6.547

[132] Gringras, P., Green, D., Wright, B., Rush, C., Sparrowhawk, M., Pratt, K., Allgar, V., Hooke, N., Moore, D., & Zaiwalla, Z. (2014). Weighted blankets and sleep in autistic children—a randomized controlled trial. Pediatrics, 134(2), 298-306. https://doi.org/10.1542/peds.2013-4285

[133] Schleien, S. J., Miller, K. D., Walton, G., & Roth, A. (2014). Connecting people with disabilities and the non-disabled through sports. Therapeutic Recreation Journal, 48(4), 296-316. https://doi.org/10.18666/trj-2014-v48-i4-4444

[134] McDonnell, J., & Dearden, A. (2021). Peer-mediated interventions to support inclusive education for students with autism spectrum disorders. Review Journal of Autism and Developmental Disorders, 8(3), 330-342. https://doi.org/10.1007/s40489-021-00245-w

About the Author

Veronica Crafton has been dedicated to working with children with autism for nearly 20 years. Throughout her career, she has developed a comprehensive skill set and knowledge base, enabling her to work with children across the autism spectrum. She began her career at the Emory Autism Center, where she implemented play therapy with preschool-aged children. Veronica later worked at The Marcus Autism Center, specializing in autism and other developmental disabilities, focusing on children with severe language delays and challenging behaviors. For six years, she served as a teacher for children with intellectual and behavioral disabilities, primarily autism, in the Cobb County School District, earning recognition as Teacher of the Year in 2013. She holds a Bachelor of Arts in Psychology and a Master of Education in Multiple and Severe Disabilities from Georgia State University and became a Board-Certified Behavior Analyst (BCBA) in 2020.

With her varied experience, Veronica is well-equipped to educate and support children, families, and educators. She is trained to work with children of diverse ages (from 2 to 18 years) and cognitive levels (from mildly to profoundly intellectually disabled). Her experience in the public school system has provided her with insight into the needs of teachers and students. In the private sector, she developed individualized educational and social goals for her clients by providing applied behavior analysis (ABA) services. Veronica's firsthand understanding of the challenges faced by families with children with autism fuels her dedication to meeting the needs of each family she serves.

In efforts to make a greater impact in the autism community, Veronica founded Amazingly Uplifted (AU).

Since 2013 AU has provided a variety of services aimed at supporting children with autism, developmental disabilities, and behavioral challenges, along with their families and educators. The organization offers educational consulting for preschools, public, private, and charter schools. Amazingly Uplifted offers professional development for educators, covering topics like behavior modification, data collection, inclusive teaching, and classroom management. Their training is interactive and practical, tailored to meet the specific needs of students and classrooms. For parents, the organization has launched a monthly training program covering topics like behavior challenges, advocacy, and family matters, aiming to build an informed and supportive community for families of children with autism. Overall, Amazingly Uplifted aims to create a supportive community where families, teachers, and children with autism can thrive and achieve their full potential.

Veronica is also an alumna of Lead Atlanta, a leadership development and community education program for young professionals and has served on multiple non-profit boards. She was also recognized in Georgia Trend's 2018 "40 Under 40" list and currently serves in the children's ministry at her local church.